China: A Journey into Its Musical Art

Chinese Music Monograph Series

ISSN: 1071-5649

Series Editors:
Yuan-Yuan Lee Ph.D.
Sin-yan Shen Ph.D.

- CHINESE MUSIC AND ORCHESTRATION: *A Primer on Principles and Practice*
- CHINESE MUSICAL INSTRUMENTS
- CHINA: *A Journey into Its Musical Art*
- WHAT MAKES CHINESE MUSIC CHINESE? *Theory, Compositions and Analysis*
- MUSICIANS OF CHINESE MUSIC
- THE REGIONAL MUSIC OF CHINA
- CHINESE MUSIC IN THE 20TH CENTURY

China: A Journey into Its Musical Art

SIN-YAN SHEN

Chinese Music Society of North America
Chicago USA

CHINA: A JOURNEY INTO ITS MUSICAL ART

First Edition, 2000
First Printing, 2000

Published in the United States of America by the Chinese Music Society of North America, P.O. Box 5275, Woodridge IL 60517-0275 USA.
http://ChineseMusic.Net

Library of Congress Catalog Card Number 00-022104

Library of Congress Cataloging in Publication Data

Shen, Sin-yan 1949-
China: a journey into its musical art / Sin-yan Shen.
p. cm. -- (Chinese Music Monograph Series)
Includes bibliographical references and index.
ISBN 1-880464-07-1
1. Music--China--History and criticism. 2. Music--China--Philosophy and aesthetics.
I. Title. II. Series.

ML336 .S463 2000
780'.951--dc21

00-022104

Bibliographical references and Index

Chinese Music Monograph Series books, the Chinese Music international journal, music full scores, sheet music, instrumental instruction books, recordings and other educational material are available from the Chinese Music Society of North America, National Headquarters, P.O. Box 5275, Woodridge IL 60517-0275 USA. Tel: 630-910-1551 FAX: 630-910-1561 http://ChineseMusic.Net

Contents

Preface

On my concert tours in North America and in Europe and on other tours with the Chinese Classical Orchestra and the Silk & Bamboo Ensemble, many friends in the audience have asked very similar questions about Chinese music. In the informance that I usually do on university campuses I have spoken at length about the musical background of the repertoire. Students and faculties have found these comments very useful. I have included many of the topics I discussed here. Thus much of this book was really written on tour.

To provide a good perspective of where I was coming from, the introductory chapters offer a brief background of my own encounters and upbringing. These include my childhood experience with theatrical music and training in the Chinese fiddles. Chapter by chapter after that we take you on a journey into dance music, opera music, ballad singing, instrumental music and vocal music.

The early development and very early systematic advances in Chinese philosophy and mathematics form the intellectual foundation of the Chinese musical system. The quest for meaning of existence by Chinese musical philosophers focused on (1) the importance of communication between one another and commitments to contribution to society, and (2) the human position in the cosmic world. Their cosmic view was the basis for universal resonance and harmony. The Chinese system of harmonic intervals is both physically just and culturally harmonious. The physical universe and the reality of acoustical systems provided practical enlightenment about resonance and harmony. Temperament theory on silk strings were developed by acoustical physicists and mathematicians. Such advances were spurred by incredible engineering and technological/industrial advances. It was on silk strings that the Chinese musicians first practiced in the world just and physically harmonious intervals. Without the strength of the silk industry perhaps much of string acoustics would have been delayed. The fascinating tones of silk strings also presented themselves as assets for expression.

It was not until the late Tang period and the Song period that the central position of the cosmic view slowly disintegrated. The Song period spelled disaster for musical aesthetics as China plunges into serious political retreat. I included significant discussion about this period and about the succeeding Yuan dynasty. The connection between Chinese bowed fiddles and the use of horse-haired bows in Europe is established.

Material for the Chinese Music Monograph Series (CMMS) has been developed over the years teaching at the graduate and the undergraduate levels and at the Research Institute of the Chinese Music Society of North America (CMSNA).

Pursuing our exploration of the almost limitless caverns of Chinese music and orchestration, so much of which has never yet come to the knowledge of the rest of the world, we approach the subject from both the angles of principles and practice. Functional discussions of musical interest, cultural molding of musical psychology, instrumental effects and acoustics are emphasized. The exploration centers on the principle of cultural acoustics, that is, the impacts of musical acoustics is strongly modified by our ear and brain which are products of culture.

The intended audience are students of music at the university level, and music practitioners. The book is written so that it requires no prior knowledge of Chinese music or acoustics. Also, no knowledge of the Chinese language is assumed.

Within this volume we find ourselves at a focal point in the present exposition: What Makes Chinese Music Chinese? The cultural preference of harmony, and thus intervals and tones and rhythms used in music, distinguishes one music from another. Chinese music, however, is unique in its uninterrupted history of more than 8000 years and very early development of theoretical systematics, acoustical and material science, and orchestral practice.

It is a pleasure to offer public gratitude to those who have shaped this work. Throughout this research and writing, Dr. Yuan-Yuan Lee provided detailed and thought-provoking critique of the discussion concerning every concept and every analysis. Colleagues in theory, composition, and performance throughout the world had stimulated the writing and completion of this text. The masters of Chinese music and acoustical masters throughout the ages inspired my theoretical and practical approach.

I specially thank my parents for without their constant encouragements and guidance over the years this work would not have been possible, and without the open-minded cultural environment provided by them in my youth the subject of cultural acoustics would not have appeared.

Prelude

Whether you are someone interested in appreciating music, a dancer, a painter, a poet, a composer, an opera singer, an instrumentalist, or a pop song singer, China has had a great deal of influence on your art form. Years ago when the world knew China only from a distance, the Chinese Music Society started to establish a strong base of musicians and music lovers in North America and Europe[1] with a common goal to elevate the understanding of the music making process and interactions between the music of different cultural systems. We approached music of the Chinese people from the angles of both "Music" and "Cultural Acoustics". Cultural Acoustics has since become a major field of study for understanding the different ways of doing things (the preference) in the world of music of different cultural systems. Our approach is deep-rooted in musical culture and answers all questions based on the most fundamental inquiry of "What Music Really Is?" It thus breaks down all cultural barriers, and all music lovers and musicians involved became messengers and recipients of the intrinsic inner musical message.

---

[1] The Chinese Music International Network (CMIN) was established 1969, and the Chinese Music Society of North America (CMSNA) was founded 1976 in the United States.

Here in the Chinese Music Monograph Series we deal in a fun-filled manner the whole range of musical arts. Dance and opera are such natural topics to begin with, so we initiate our musical journey on these incredibly powerful yet grassroots art forms. Hand, eye, body, and steps have captured our fancy in Chinese regional and classical dances. These aspects of movements in dance are equally important, on each dancer in each dance. The captivating "vocal styles", virtual reality and drum beats in free tempo, of the Chinese regional theaters and the Peking Opera, have inspired the inner desires of many to get onto the stage and permanently stay on there. Chinese art music and folk music are such involved areas, that we slowly but surely get involved in the basic philosophy, so that the underlying thinking process behind music making, as well as the great minds behind the incredible musical creations, can be properly introduced. In some areas we deal in slightly more technical details, because they happen to be areas where you can efficiently achieve significant depth without too much trouble. In all areas you will gather enough interest and knowledge to want to become a more specialized appreciator. The area of the Chinese orchestras is, of course, more exhaustively covered in other writings (for a primer on the subject see *Chinese Music & Orchestration: A Primer on Principles and Practice*). However, the artistic and aesthetic aspects of the music of the Chinese orchestras is quite completely explored on this all encompassing journey, so that if you are a composer type, the information here is useful for your composition efforts. In addition to the orchestral chapters here, more complete analysis of the reeded wind, percussion, silk plucked strings, and silk bowed strings can be found in the volume *Chinese Musical Instruments*.

For all readers, to start with, you do not need to have any formal acoustical training. You also do not have to know what precisely are the musical intervals. Most people do know something about the octave. That is quite a wide interval. You will find that two notes that are an octave apart sound like they are in unison, when they are played at the same time. When you cut the octave in half (both physically and musically), you get what is called the "fifth" (because for example from "do" to "sol" there are five steps, similarly from "re" to "la", and from "mi" to "ti", where the regular scale would be do, re, mi, fa, sol, la, ti). Please note that in this series, for simplicity, we sometimes abbreviate "sol" to "so". Two notes that are a fifth apart, when played together, do not sound like they are in unison as was the case of the octave sounding together, but you hear a chord here a simple and harmonious one. That's a fifth - try to get used to it on the piano or the guitar. When you cut the fifth in half. You have either a major third or a minor third, and a major third is "wider" than a minor third. Smaller than the thirds are the seconds.... The primary difference between musical systems of different culture is their individual preference for intervals, and thus producing a difference in the breadth of their harmonic system.

What is in a harmonic system? In all compositions, there are intentional conflicts between harmony and discord. But what is harmonic and what is not is extremely culture-specific. In present-day European and American music the second is a discord, while it is musically harmonic in China.

Here we are dealing with specific intervals, but in reality it always is the total combined effect of many intervals, while your brain still remembers them, whether they be sounding at the same time or slightly apart, that causes your brain to be stimulated in desired fashion. In the performance of a single instrument, such harmonic stimulation comes into play in the interaction between the player and the instrument - thus his or her tone. Frequently musicians do not think of the tone as a harmonic entity but it absolutely is. The cultural acoustical preferences of a race or a nationality determines the types of tone of instruments it accepts. This explains why certain instruments sound Chinese, whether you are familiar with it or not. However, with a Chinese instrument, the way you play it can still make it sound utterly bland and thus not Chinese - one example is to ask a violin player to play the *erhu*. Without becoming accustomed to the acoustical resonances of the *erhu*, the violin player may think it is just another string instrument on which you are to divide the strings. The *erhu* and the violin are wildly different instruments in that the performance of the *erhu* actually requires the production of acoustics that maximizes the contrast between its major resonance components, whereas the philosophy behind the development of the violin was even out register differences as much as possible.

Chinese music is built on a totally consistent harmonic system which controls melodic progression, orchestration, and temperament use. It is perhaps the only major musical system in the world that has such all-encompassing requirements on all aspects of its music, and at the same time allowing the largest flexibility in the acceptance of harmonic intervals into music. In the 1960s and the early 1970s through the work at the Chinese Music Society of North America, we discovered the cyclical harmonic skeletons known as *zhi, shang, yu, jue, gong* in the Chinese harmonic system. Before this work, those terms were for a long time referred to as scale steps. Even the Encyclopedia Britannica had it wrong, until I corrected them. This set of harmony with implied harmonic skeletons is self generating, always in tune without equalizing temperaments because its system does not believe in the twelve tones alone. The same harmonic intervals which are the basis of the Chinese harmonic system were found to appear prominently in the design of the overtone structure of the Chinese musical instruments. The same harmonic intervals which are the basis of the Chinese harmonic system were used in the design of the ancient dual-pitched bronze *zhong* bells[2] (see Shen, 1987. The *zhong* is a musical bell while the *bo* bell is a ceremonial bell), and in the design of Chinese silk and bamboo musical instruments, and in particular, is the basis for string tuning on the *qin*[3] (the fingerboard zither

---

[2] The *zhong* bell is quite special. The complete bell chime may consist of several dozen *zhong* bells, each producing two different notes - sounds crazy? It's an acoustical miracle by design. The chime is collectively called *bianzhong* (the bell set).

[3] The *qin* is another crazy instrument. Most of the music written for it has no timing marks. Each time the music is played, it has to be musically

with seven strings and a range of five octaves), the *sanxian* (the fingerboard lute with three strings and no frets), the *zheng* (the horizontal open-string zither), the *pipa* (the grand lute), the *erhu* (the second fiddle), the *tuoyin erhu* (the supporting second fiddle), the *matouqin* (the horse head fiddle), the *zhuihu* (the fingerboard vertical fiddle), the *jinghu* (the soprano fiddle of Beijing Opera), the *banhu* (the wood fiddle of the Chinese orchestra and the Clapper Operas), the *liuqin* (the mandolin), and the *ruan* (the ancient round lute) family.

You will find an emphasis, in this volume of the Chinese Music Monograph Series, on the important Spring & Autumn period (770-476 BC), when the level of intellectual exchange was at its height in Chinese civilization. The Spring & Autumn period and the Warring States period make up what is called the Eastern Zhou, which was the second part of the Zhou period. The first part of the Zhou was Western Zhou (11th Century-770 BC). In the 1970s we were able to, in great detail, separate the musical bells from the non-musical bells of the Shang-Zhou periods. We studied complete overtone structure of all existing Shang (16th-11th Century BC) and Zhou (11th Century-221 BC) bells and was delighted to find the acoustical design of bells of each period, and in particular in the case of the *zhong* musical bells established direct connection between the choice of their

---

interpreted. The result is timeless music, that can have a life in any given dynasty, when the artistic preferences on tempo and rhythmic elements may be different from the preferences of other periods. Its music is thus truly timeless.

overtone structure and the Chinese harmonic system as we know it today.

You will also find that I had few good things to say about the Song period (960-1279), especially the second part known as the Southern Song period (1127-1279), when as evident from their composition, almost all musicians were desperate about China's political future, for China's leaders had decided to take the path of historical decline.

Until very recently when western orchestral scores arrived, Chinese instrumental music was never fully notated, allowing for embellishments and variation according to players and environment, while orchestral scores permitted even greater extent of improvised performance. Thus sometime our silk and bamboo is called Shanghai jazz in the west. In reality it's not just silk and bamboo that improvises; Across the board Chinese ensemble music and solo music are among the most improvised in the world. The art of improvisation has been around for so long in China that most people do not pay special attention to it. The general concept begins with the timeless notations whereby a "dapu" process is used to determine what goes into the performance. I have called these scores "timeless" as they permit the fullest transmittal of a composition in time, through drastically different stylistic periods. This is possible primarily due to the importance of interval relations in Chinese compositions. Classical composition such as the "Lao Liuban" (Old Six Measure) merely provides the framework of interval series for the work. Embellishments and substitutions of individual notes by other members of the harmony used at the specific point in the "score".

REFERENCES

Lee, Yuan-Yuan and Shen Sin-yan, *Chinese Musical Instruments*, Chinese Music Society of North America, Chicago (1999).

Shen, Sinyan, Acoustics of Ancient Chinese Bells, *Scientific American*, **256**, 94 (1987).

Shen, Sin-yan, *Chinese Music and Orchestration: A Primer on Principles and Practice*, Chinese Music Society of North America, Chicago (1991).

■

Chinese Culture & China's Musical Art

The variety of China's musical art is absolutely fabulous. To people who have come into contact with Chinese music, it is sometimes difficult to grasp the full picture. On this journey you will travel with me into the most exciting world of all forms of China's musical art. Chinese culture is treated as a whole here, as I understand it. I want to tell you in the beginning what we are about to do and why we are doing it the way we do. We will travel into China's past, explore all of its present day regions that have produced the fascinating music and philosophically different musical art forms, follow how the world has interacted with China in musical art and culture, and gain personal insights into what makes Chinese music Chinese and what makes it so fascinating?

Most importantly, on this journey we will experience the inner workings of the music making process, whether it be that of dance music, theatrical music, ballad singing, vocal music, or instrumental music. Remember - those are the major categories of Chinese music art.

The 20th Century was when the West came to know the most about China historically, and yet the last part of it was also when much of China's civilization was compressed[1] with the highest rate of compression[2], while we witness never-seen-before high speeds of information flow, thus making a deep understanding of any aspect of China somewhat difficult[3]. We hope to solve this specific problem here with respect to the broad topic of the musical art of the Chinese people. Our approach is a cultural one, and we'll go about it by always answering first the very basic question "What music really is?" If time slices of China's culture were imbedded into a series of time capsules, we would indeed have the possibility of taking a vertical journey into China's musical art. This trip into China's past would have provided a true picture of the evolutions of the music-making

---

[1] An unprecedented progress in human history took place beginning in 1994 when the wave of internet-related information technology took charge of information flow in societies. This progress has made accessible great amount of information not previously as readily available to the general public. For Chinese culture, however, it has meant a serious compression of its historical events on world stage. This happens to be the case, first because much of China's historical literature is not yet available broadly to the outside world, and secondly because citizens in the internet age are, relatively speaking, less patient and demand quick and short answers to any question, thus sometimes getting very shallow answers.

[2] As the great Studs Terkel would say, regarding the state of present day communication, "We are more and more into communications and less into communication."

[3] Near the end of the second millennium, USA Today featured the headline "Asian History a Mystery to Americans". This is caused first by a general lack of good information on Asia, and secondly by a "rush mentality" in getting any information *fast* towards the end of the 20th Century and into the 21st.

process of the Chinese, and no arguments need be made regarding what is more traditional[4] than others, because the process itself has always been an evolution, with fairly frequent quantum jumps in the process, making it a highly creative process. Today many scholars could no longer follow the intricate threads that wove China's past, and their work often merely focused either on a comparison between the present and something they call the past, or on the comparison between a compressed China and something they call the West. While the lack of proper time representation in the rapid information flow is taking place, much of the outside world's battle with China's very different philosophy[5] is now being brought to the surface, and is contributing to new modes of contact at the frontier of present day international interaction. China is different and, historically, China led in everything that supported music[6].

---

[4] "What makes up traditional music?" is a constant topic of argument since the 1950s among Chinese scholars and between Chinese and Western scholars. As a result, "What is more traditional?" also became a keen topic of discussion.

[5] Chinese philosophy governs the way musicians deal with music, the way writers write, and painters paint. Since the later parts of the 19th Century, the West has struggled without success in quantifying and categorizing the many behaviors of the Chinese. Music, however, is one clear place where they have had the most battles with Chinese philosophy.

[6] The history of Chinese musical instruments has been a history of new resonator discovery, new use of physiology in acoustical excitation, and musical acoustics. Acoustical research in the 20th Century revealed a most distinguished history of the science of music in China. Ancient China possessed a level of acoustical science that was essential in supporting the elaborate musical art of

Chinese culture is unique, but I have found its music to be spectacular, in both scope and content, and especially in the modes of communication of its music. But best of all, the study of China's musical art offers vantage points for looking at the many conceptual turns in human philosophy and civilization, as China actually touched all of our lives in the world at various different points in time.

The beginning of my journey into China's music had been to answer questions, questions that had bothered the outside world for a very long time. For some time the outside world focused on China's musical scale, thus the pentatonic studies and the pentatonic competitions, which turned up nothing. As it turns out, scale is somewhat of a western concept. The Chinese went by harmony, thus several songs with distinctly different melodic lines may sound totally different to the outside world, but they sound the same to the Chinese, because, as a thorough analysis will tell you, their melodic lines were formed by members of the very same "series of harmonies". A famed class of music like "The Old Six Measures" thus offer the harmonic framework for composition. Thus the Chinese hears harmonies rather than melodies. I first encountered the problems of understanding China's music when I became entangled in the web of inconsistent literature regarding the use of the terms *gong*,

---

those periods. Physics and engineering worked hand in hand to perfect musical instruments and to arrive at desirable orchestration. These are accomplishments that have modern counterparts. In contrast, the overall design of a large set of dual-pitch bells for the performance of music is an achievement that has no equal in the modern physics of music.

shang, *jue*, *zhi*, and *yu*. I will tell you right away - something you should remember - that *zhi* is the most common harmony in Chinese music. In literatures from the west and in literature written by recent Chinese scholars, the terms were by error referred to as scale steps. Such references, however, were nowhere to be found in Chinese classical music texts. In the musical practices of "xuangong" which means rotating the gong, and "zhuandiao" which mean changing the modality, we encounter their true meaning. For solving this problem, I devoted part of the 1960s and the early part of the 1970s in a unified study of the Chinese musical system. When the many parts of a musical system are looked upon together, you begin to understand the system's inner working. In studying the music making processes of the Han Chinese and of all the minority groups, I was struck by the coherence and unity of their harmonic preferences through the Chinese musical system. All regional music and all ethnic music were found in our study to be integral subsets of the Chinese musical system. The unification of China's music apparently was arrived at a very long time ago, so long ago that the regional music of China and the ethnic music of China all became subsystems of the Chinese musical system. I was told by one of the visiting Chinese scholars to the United States in the late 1970s that this result of our research was what Chinese politicians should be studying, as many of them were seeking rationalization of their belief that China should be united once again, but with no success. The answer is truly a cultural one. As China and the world seek to understand each other once again in the 21st Century, what we go through in this journey into China's musical art offers important points of departure from focusing merely on immediately relevant items in our day to day international interactions.

My Journey into China's Musical Art

My own journey in the study of Chinese musical art started in vocal music and the story-telling aspects of ballad singing at a very early age. My love at the time was in folk songs and art songs. Instrumental music and ensemble music then dominated the rest of my life as many of you now know. During this later period of immersion in instrumental and ensemble music I returned to theatrical singing and theatrical orchestration, and learned the vocal and instrumental components of ballad singing. The music, mostly ensemble and orchestral, which dominates my thoughts, includes a large class of dance music, both folk and theatrical. Thus all in all, incredible as it may sound, I took an artistic and mental journey into China's musical art. To put it simply, the musical art of China as we know it falls into (A) vocal music, (B) instrumental music, (C) ballad singing, (D) theatrical music, and (E) dance music. My own growth was primarily in the philosophy of music making.

Of all the musical art forms of China, the most highly developed is chamber instrumental music - another thing you will encounter all the time and you should remember. Worldwide, the art form of chamber instrumental music started in China and it includes a very large category of solo music and ensemble music. China is the civilization in which pure instrumental music as art music was recognized very early. Almost all Chinese classical music has its roots in pure instrumentals of the scholarly community during the Shang-Zhou era. The major developments in pure instrumental artistry occurred on silk strings. By the end of the Song period, however, these classical music had seriously declined. In the Shang and Zhou period pure instrumental music was the sought-after art form among elite musicians and scholars. This early development had to do with very early systematic advances in Chinese philosophy and mathematics. Chinese philosophers constantly asked themselves the meaning of existence, and in their quest they focused on two levels: (1) the importance of communication between one another and commitments to contribution to society, and (2) the human position in the cosmic world. The cosmic point of view was indeed central to serious music making. It was not until the late Tang[7] period and the Song period that the central position of the cosmic view slowly disintegrated. The physical universe and the reality of acoustical systems also

---

[7] The Tang period (618-907) was a most prosperous period in China. All neighboring countries looked up to the Tang court for leadership. Late Tang, however, was another story. The short Five Dynasties and Ten Kingdom period (907-979) soon followed. The Song court was established in 960, forty years before the beginning of the last millennium. Northern Song (960-1127) ended with defeat, and Southern Song (1127-1279) was considered one of the most sorry times in Chinese history. This continual decline obviously affected artists, scholars and poets, as cosmic scheme of things were replaced by outbursts of deep sorrow.

enlightened musicians. Temperament theory on silk[8] strings were developed by acoustical physicists and mathematicians in China. Such advances were spurred by engineering and technological/industrial advances. It was on silk strings that the Chinese musicians first practiced in the world just and physically harmonious intervals. Without the strength of the silk industry perhaps much of string acoustics would have been delayed. The fascinating tones of silk strings also presented themselves as assets for expression. In the everyday life of scholar musicians, the importance of commitments to friendship and musical expressions in such relationships paralleled the importance of literary expressions. Vocal music accompanied by instruments later became a minor component of this main stream of pure instrumental music. Throughout those early days, the Chinese explored with all acoustical material and invented all classes of resonators, on which instrumental music were composed. During Shang and Zhou China, musical art was supported by the rapid developments in science and technology. During the 1970s I studied the interaction between the scientists and engineers and the musical artists during the Spring & Autumn period. I found the level of their interaction to be much higher than the level of support of music by the science and technology community in the 20th Century. The Spring & Autumn period in China was perhaps unique. Dozens of principalities as regional powers were

---

[8] Silk was the strongest industrial fibre in the world. The silk industry was invented by the Chinese, and Chinese musicians were the first to learn a great about the acoustics of the string because the silk industry was in place so early.

competing for military might and economic prosperity, and in turn compete for the best human talents, in diplomacy, in military strategy, in management, in mathematics, in technology, and in music and the arts. During this extraordinary time, China experienced the largest intellectual advances in its history. These intellectual advances translated into practical advances for everyday life. In the courts, musicians aimed for the ideal instrumental groupings for orchestration, and the presence of advanced knowledge of acoustics and material science supported this desire in earnest. In my years of study of the acoustics of the Shang-Zhou dual-pitched bronze bells, the concept of nodal lines was found to be already well and alive three millenniums ago[9]. The early appearance of u-tube design in wind instruments, and the dual pitch design of *zhong* bells in bell chimes are obvious examples of milestone advances in instrumental design and acoustical understanding.

With this understanding, my research in music in the last thirty some years centered on the unified field of temperaments, acoustics, orchestration, and musical psychology. Believe it or not,

---

[9] The history of Chinese musical instruments has been a history of new resonator discovery, new use of physiology in acoustical excitation, and musical acoustics. Acoustical research in the 20th Century revealed a most distinguished history of the science of music in China. Ancient China possessed a level of acoustical science that was essential in supporting the elaborate musical art of those periods. Physics and engineering worked hand in hand to perfect musical instruments and to arrive at desirable orchestration. These are accomplishments that have modern counterparts. In contrast, the overall design of a large set of dual-pitch bells for the performance of music is an achievement that has no equal in the modern physics of music.

these subjects are actually very closely and intimately related. The division of octaves or the division of twelves, which ever the case may be, is a specific culture's preference in sonic sequences, and musical intervals. Such preference is used to support the choice of overtones in instrumental voices and tone qualities. Such preference also supports the tuning of strings and winds and percussions. Such preference manifests in instrumental voice combinations and orchestration, and such preference is the basis for the positive musical psychology of the audience. My ultimate objective was to be able to explain music to listeners, performers and composers. The field of cultural acoustics was born. My process of understanding took many years. It was, however, through countless performances and lectures, through constant interaction with musicians of different backgrounds, that my own thinking matured.

My love for theatrical music brought me deep into the area of vocal language, of inflections and styles of verbal and musical expressions. These expressions are very much present in numerous *erhu* and other fiddle compositions, and in folk instrumental music. For political reasons, some scholars like to overemphasize the distinction between folk and classical music. In my own thinking, these music are so closely related in cultural acoustics, that their distinction only appears when different sectors of society play them. Social differences dominate the superficial appearance of a specific type of music. Dialect and ethnic differences further dominate the superficial appearance of a region's music. In my unified analysis, I found Chinese music to be one and the same system, from North to South, and from East to West. It is the Chinese system of harmony that dominates and links the music of all Chinese people. The system spills over to many other civilizations, but remains the broadest in harmonic interval acceptance in the world. The unified acoustical basis of all Chinese music has not only unified the musical culture of the provinces, but also the large number of ethnic groups. Chinese music has been a great source of inspiration[10] for other civilizations that had been in contact with China. It has also been a significant and large positive systematic influence on the music of its neighbors and friends.

On this journey I provide a critique of what happened musically in China. Spring & Autumn (770-476 BC) was an unprecedented period in human civilization when talents and human resources were put to use in the most important creative endeavors. Major principalities competed for these artists, scholars, diplomates, and engineers. The rise of the science of acoustics supported the ever-increasing requirements in the art of music making. Art music was at the center of the Chinese musical system. Music for court and dance were a minor part of this philosophical mainstream. The decline of art music started in the Wei Jin periods, and art music was gone by the second part of the Song dynasty. Musically we have very little good things to say about the Song. The only good thing that happened in the

---

[10] The most important being the spread in resonators and acoustical systems, e.g. the free-reed and the clamped reed systems, and the many coupled system and the u-tube. The introduction of fiddles with horse-haired bows is an inspiration for a whole class of instruments - the present day bowed strings.

Song period was the building-up of the scenic city of Hangzhou. When the Song imperial capital of Kaifeng[11] was taken over by the Nuzhen nomads from the north in the 1120s, the Song dynasty migrated to Hangzhou, taking with it over one million artists, merchants, officials, scholars, servants and slaves to the city on water[12].

During the Han through the Sui-Tang periods, the pear-shaped lutes took prominence across the Asia-Asia Minor continent. The resonator of the pear-shaped lutes linked plucked strings with the violin family. The story of Marco Polo linked Chinese fiddles with the new string music of Europe which today is the basis of the fundamental spectrum of the modern symphony.

---

[11] Kaifeng was in the 11th Century the greatest city on earth. Its population was close to a million. Today a significant population of Chinese Jews still live in this ancient city of Kaifeng, now in Henan Province.

[12] The other famous city on water is Suzhou, another center of music.

The Art of Chinese Dances: Expressions Using Hand, Eye, Body, and Steps

Visitors to China who are fortunate enough to take part in dance activities have always been fascinated[1] and impressed by the range of different expressions in Chinese dance. Chinese dance movements employ a large range of hand (including fingers) and eye expressions which are unknown to the west. To appreciate these colorful art forms, one needs a good perspective on the philosophy of Chinese dance as an art, and a technical understanding of its expressions. Chinese dance is characterized by several integral parts. To put it simply, you may want to specially observe the following aspects of Chinese dance expression as a whole and on every dancer: (1) hands, (2) eyes, (3) body, (4) mode, and (5) steps[2]. These aspects of movements in dance, which I call the integral parts of a Chinese dance, are equally important, on each dancer in each dance. Hand movements, eye focus, body direction, and steps all follow a

[1] The finger and eye language is seldom seen in the west.

[2] Chinese dance theory has these specific terms, but it is more important to get a feel of what exactly to pay attention to and understand how it all fits together to deliver an artistic message.

chosen mode of expression[3]. The combination of these five aspects expresses an emotion and tells a story in abstract reality. In "Tea Picking" dance[4], for instance, no prop is ever used, and yet for the captivated audience, the dancers go uphill, go downhill, pass through a bridge, arrive at the hilly tea orchard, pick teas, and communicate constantly along the way with each other. All parts of this sequence are accomplished expressively without the audience seeing a physical hill, a physical bridge, or an orchard. The abstraction is effectively performed by dance sequences involving all of the five integral parts we outlined above. Many of these parts also appear in the art of Chinese operas, but accomplished with much less dancing, but with highly skilled singing, acting, recitation and sometimes acrobatics. Both Chinese dance and Chinese theater rely heavily on live ensemble accompaniment that is improvised within a well known framework[5], as a result the ensemble or orchestral music associated with the dance performance or the theatrical

---

[3] Hand and eye expressions are much better developed in Chinese dance than perhaps in dances of any other country.

[4] The popular dance "Caicha Pu Die" (Picking Tea Leaves and Catching Butterflies) which the China Performing Arts Company performed in Europe in 1957 is a "Tea Picking" dance. The popular orchestral music "Caicha Deng" (Tea Picking Lantern) is from a lantern dance.

[5] Every one performing knows what to expect, but no one knows exactly how every note will be played, with what level of repetition, and at what specific speed. Such improvisation according to the movement of the whole company and specific audience environment creates an element of surprise all the time and makes the performance exciting and audience excited.

Warring States period (5th Century BC) dancers dance while playing stone chimes which are called *bianqing* (set of *qing* musical stones).

performance often have their own instrumental repertoire as well.

The famous "Ya Wu" in the ancient dynasties is the ceremonial dance to celebrate the Emperor's civil and military accomplishments. "Wen Wu" is the civil dance with dancers holding *yue* panpipe and pheasant feather, while "Wu Wu" is the military dance with dancers holding shields and hatchets. Ceremonial dances in the early Western Zhou period (11th Century BC) which originated from six earlier periods included the "Rose-Colored Cloud" from the time of the Yellow Emperor. The dance is named for the clouds said to have risen in the sky when Yellow Emperor united the different Chinese people and founded the Chinese nation.

During the Han period (206 BC - 220 AD) and the Sui and Tang periods (7th to 10th Century) we saw the height of Chinese classical dance and folk dance when they were integrated into court dances. The Han court had the most powerful Music Ministry, called the Yuefu, in history. The Music Ministry was responsible for collecting folk songs and dances. During the reign of the Han Emperor WuDi, in 141-87 BC, the Music Ministry formally established dances that were popular in the separate State principalities during the Warring States period (475-221 BC). The Ministry brought together 829 artists on its payroll, including 142 students in training. Chinese dance and music in the Han court was impressive then. During WuDi's time, music and dance from Western China, on the silk route, were included. Such cultures as from present-day Xinjiang and

The Zenghou Yi bell chime from the Warring States period (5th Century BC) is the best known bell chime because of our acoustical and musical studies, and is here played by a musician/dancer.

the whole area west of the Gansu Corridor were popular in the Han court. Most influential were dances from the oasis kingdom of Kucha in today's Xinjiang. Dances in Northern Zhou (6th Century) through Sui and Tang periods were performed to Kucha's rhythmic dance music. Also included were music and dances from India and Koryo (part of the Korean peninsula).

The political stability and economic prosperity of the Tang period (618 - 907) set the stage for another boom in Chinese dance. The artists of the Tang court, drawing on the music and dance of the previous dynasties, were classified by performance into ten types. Li Shimin, the Tang Emperor TaiZong, popularized the dances "Prince Qin Storms the Enemy

Lines" and "Jubilant Celebration", to which he personally contributed to the composition of the music. During the reign of Emperor XuanZong, in 712 - 796, the famous dances under the category "Rainbow Skirt & Feather Cape" were popular. The original "The Moon on High", one of the best known Chinese classical orchestral music, was popular during this time.

The rise of the opera as the most popular art form at the end of the Song period and through the Yuan Period[6] (1271-1368) brought about the decline in dance. During the Ming and the Qing periods, there were very few professional dancers, but dances remained a festival activity in cities and villages.

Things were different in the 20th Century. Large-scale efforts in collecting folk and classical dances took place beginning in the 1950s. Professional choreographers and professional composers joined hands to produce some of the most colorful productions. In the second half of the 20th Century, large scale popular dances we are all familiar with include "Red Ribbon Dance", "Lotus Dance", and "Peacock Dance". The dance drama "The Dagger Society" from Shanghai has also been very popular, and it included the famous "Bow Dance". The Dagger Society composed by Shang Yi and made popular by the Shanghai Dance Theater is not only well known for its many dance pieces, it is also extremely popular for its orchestral masterpieces.

---

[6] During Yuan times, cities became centers of commerce and musical art was becoming commercialized. The citizen wanted entertainment, and what resulted was a boom in theater (It was like everybody wanted to go see the movies).

Favorite first movement passage of The Bow Dance from "The Dagger Society" by Shang Yi

Chinese loves to dance. Dance is one of the most important activities during any festivity and many ceremonies. This happens in every province. For visitors to China, the farmer's dance known as "Yangge" (A "yang" is a rice seedling, and "ge" is a song or music; "yangge" is the group dance by farmers to celebrate their hard work in the field) is frequently encountered. In fact in large cities such as Beijing, senior citizens gather every night for Yangge. In this case it is both an exercise and a social gathering[7]. There are northern Yangge and southern Yangge. The most popular form in China today is the

---

[7] In Beijing, you will find lively ladies telling you that they do the Yangge "twist".

northern Yangge. A Yangge performance in a farming community is spectacular. The orchestra walks with the dancers playing easily recognized Yangge music. Yangge music is highly rhythmic and very simple. The dancers however take intricate hand, eye, step, and body movements. Popular northern Yangge can be grouped into Northern Shaanxi Yangge, Northeastern Yangge, Hebei Di-Yangge, Shandong Jiaozhou Yangge (from Jiaozhou area), and Guzi Yangge (Drum Yangge). Each has its own style and characteristics. In most cases, dances are playing different characters, holding fans, handkerchief, and silk brocade. Structurewise, the beginning and the final movements are "dachang" group parade dances, with the intermediate movements called "xiaochang" featuring specific dances with a story involving two to three dancer/players. The now famous "Red Ribbon Dance" loved by the American audience during the tour of the Chinese Performing Arts Company in 1978 is a combination of Yangge steps with silk ribbon dance. Silk ribbon dance is classical as well as folk. In 1930 when Mei Lanfang, Chinese opera superstar, conducted his first American tour. He performed from New York to San Francisco, where Chinese opera was first presented in the U.S. in 1852. He offered a program of Chinese drama "Especially Prepared for American Reception" and included his most famous long ribbon dance "The Heavenly Maiden Scattering Flowers." His performances earlier in the 20th Century provided a milestone for public knowledge of Chinese classical dances. "Red Ribbon Dance" features powerful male and female styles of ribbon dance using short ribbons and very long ribbons on a stick. It begins with male and female dancers

Out of the red torches came long and short red ribbons (Courtesy Chinese Performing Arts Company).

dancing Yangge with a red torch in their hands. All of a sudden, out of the torches came long and short red ribbons. The long ribbons are like fire dragons. This new creation is extremely exciting for any audience, and is accompanied by the Chinese orchestra. It is great fun for all, dancers and the audience. After the popularity of the "Red Ribbon Dance" in the 1978 tour, all over the world, especially in America and Europe, athletes have adopted its techniques in their own shows, e.g. for the Olympics.

The Yangge theme of the "Red Ribbon Dance" is by far the best written rendition of any Yangge theme used for a large scale dance representing China

"Silk Ribbon Dance" can be classified into "Long Ribbon" and "Short Ribbon" categories. The basic dance movements are separated into single hand ribbon dance, and two hand ribbon dance. In "Short Ribbon Dance", the dances have ribbons of length less than six feet in both hands and follows "Yangge" steps. The ribbons fly in a left-right, and then up-down motion. It is lively and free. The "Long Ribbon Dance" uses ribbon as long as 4-6 meters on 1-foot long sticks. The skillful dancer use either a single ribbon, or two ribbons, to produce all kinds of silk patterns. Another technique is to use a 10 meter silk ribbon without a stick - here the dancer puts the middle section of the silk on his or her shoulder, and controls the two halves of the silk in wavy patterns. All of these techniques are today included in the "Red Ribbon Dance".

In my travel to regional dances, I have been fascinated by the "flower lantern" known as "Huadeng". The "Huadeng" is a large class of regional dance. "Huadeng" is, literally, Flower Lantern, and has many other names. It is also known as Jumping the Lantern, Playing with the Lantern, and Lantern Theater.

"Flower Lantern" is a popular dance genre in Yunnan, Guizhou, Sichuan and their surrounding areas[8]. The dances vary from place to place, but the dancers all carry lanterns or fans. Not only do they dance, the dancers also sing. Such expressions using singing and dancing can be used in a theater, thus creating the "Huadeng Xi", the Flower Lantern Opera. "Yunnan Huadeng" of Yunnan Province, for example, has a very strong instrumental component. Many Huadeng artists are also highly accomplished instrumental players. The *yueqin* master Li Yongnian[9] of the Yunnan Huadeng Theater Company (Yunnan Huadeng Jutuan) in Kunming was one such well known figure. I have in recent times visited the same company where Li Yongnian had worked, and it is obvious that the impact of his and previous generations of flower lantern artists persist.

Lantern Dances were frequently described in Song literature. In "Dongjing Menghua Lu" (Essays on the Prosperous Eastern Capital) the Lantern Festival in the Song capital was depicted in detail: "Fifteenth day of the First Month....On both sides of the royal street, people have gathered, special shows are displayed, a hundred different theater and music and dance are performed....the music can be heard ten miles away." Other literature spoke of female dance teams performing on the main street on both the 15th and the 16th of the First Month, and the

8 All in southern, or southwestern China.

9 *Yueqin* is the general name for the moon lute, which is round. Li Yongnian's *yueqin* is the type used in Yunnan Flower Lantern music, has an octagonal resonator, and is more resonant in musical acoustics.

audience refused to leave. In the Ming period, the playwright Kong Shangren (1648-1718) in his essay about watching a huge lantern performance in the residence of Yu Jinquan. He detailed the scale of the lantern dance, the different program parts, the dance movements, and the spectacular changes in the dance pattern: "One after another the lanterns were shown....The twelve golden ladies with 24 lanterns have their faces reflecting the lantern light....enchantment rises....a hundred turns and a thousand spins....I lost count." In describing the patterns, he was fascinated by the taiji patterns, square and circular fields....the dancers were together at one point and were diffused at the next, like Lady Chang E circling the Osmanthus. Here he compared the lantern dancers with the master techniques of Madam Gongsun[10] of the Tang Dynasty. Such high praises indicate the level of Ming's lantern dances. In the Qing[11] period, lantern dances became even more popular, and 36 patterns were used to describe its variety. Ancient lantern dance were classified into the popular

---

[10] Madam Gongsun is the best known Chinese dancer from the Tang period. The poet Du Fu (712-770) was present when she performed her famed "Jian Qi" (The Energy of the Sword) in 717. In 767 Du Fu wrote about the performance: "There was a beauty named Gongsun. Her performance of "Jian Qi" shook all spaces. The audience was so shattered, that heaven and earth stayed depressed for the longest time." Madam Gongsun was in military uniform for her performance. Her style was so powerful that everyone loved her dance in military uniform.

[11] Qing (1644-1911) was the very last dynasty of China. It ended with the founding of the Chinese Republic in the successful 1911 Revolution led by Sun Yat-sen, the father of modern China.

Depiction of Madam Gongsun in sword dance by Ye Yu-zhong. Madam Gongsun is the best known sword dancer in history who danced her sword dances with or without a sword street variety and those performed in Mandarin residences. Today only the folk version is performed.

Lantern Dance is the most popular of Lantern Festival performances. It takes many forms and has many names. Their names all appear in the County Records. It goes to show how ever popular lantern dances have been historically from dynasty to dynasty.

Sword Dance is very classical. Madam Gongsun was the first famous sword dancers. Her military dance style was so powerful and convincing that she did not even need to use a sword[12]. In modern times Mei Lanfang's "Farewell My Concubine" featured the best known double sword dance in Peking Opera. Another sword dance well choreographed is in "Stealing the Magic Herb" in "The Legend of the White Serpent". Sword Dance combines martial art with dance, it utilizes the focused movements of point, poke, pick, break, stir and fend. Today Sword Dance combines sword martial art and theatrical classical sword dance, to form a more diverse and highly captivating dance art for supporting the specific characters of a dance drama or in an opera.

There is a large number of well recognized minority nationality dances which are full of color and special characteristics. The Dai dance "Peacock Dance" is from Southwestern China where the Dai nationality resides. This dance of peacocks bathing is fabulously attractive. The graceful up-down movements of the peacocks and the posture of the lead

---

[12] Here the power of abstraction rules.

"Peacock Dance" - Music by Luo Zhongrong - is a nationally recognized number depicting dance of beautiful peacocks from Southwestern China. The original theme is from the Dai nationality

peacock posing are unforgettable. Its music by Luo Zhongrong based on Dai music is now an orchestral masterpiece as well.

Against the back drop of the Old Silk Route, the Gansu Song and Dance Ensemble produced the dance drama "Along the Silk Road. Incredible variety of dances are included in this production from Western China. Dance movements based on Tang dynasty murals are beautifully choreographed.

A great number of these beautiful productions are now available on VCD.

Chinese Music
Official Publication of the Chinese Music Society of North America vol 11 no 1

On Mei Lanfang, Qi Rushan and Liu Tianhua

My father is, and has always been, an avid supporter of Peking opera. I remember when I was still very young, some of the most exciting activities in my daily life took place when he brought me to a great variety of Peking opera performances and to the opera rehearsals. It was during these events that my love for the *sanxian* (the fingerboard lute with python skin drum), the *jinghu* (the soprano bamboo fiddle), the *yueqin* (moon lute), and the *erhu*[1] first developed. My father loved the artistry of Mei Lanfang, one of the most well-known figures in Peking Opera history. When the Chinese Music Society of North America first published the picture of Mei Lanfang playing the Goddess of River Luo in the "Chinese Music" International Journal many years ago, his remarks to me included reminiscences on how much he enjoyed Mei Lanfang's performances when my grandfather took him to the shows. And with great passion he would elaborate on the vocal style and performances. So it was a family tradition to go to the opera. In this and other musical connections, I think of Mei Lanfang often. My family's love for

---

[1] The small sanxian is a very impressive fingerboard drum lute, an accompaniment instrument in the Peking opera. The jinghu is the lead high-pitched fiddle. The yueqin is the moon lute, providing percussive plucked attack in support of the singing, and the erhu plays second fiddle to the jinghu.

the musical arts and all related artistic endeavors is truly the inspiration behind my lifelong pursuit of performance[2] and musical, cultural and acoustical research.

In the late 1960s when I first arrived, the United States was under rapid transformation. The highway system became completely developed, ordinary citizens were travelling more and more around the country, and the contact between Americans and other cultures greatly increased. I became a cultural ambassador under those circumstances somewhat by default[3]. In the symphony circle, musicians were either intrigued or excited by my performances and by broad-based discussions with me about Chinese musical arts and cultural and musical acoustics. Unintentionally, I was a constant source of cultural and artistic information on Chinese music during lectures, concerts, and musical and cultural gatherings. In the major universities here, I served as a musical focal point for many local groups. In these settings, I realized, very early, that research in the Chinese musical arts was far from being taken seriously in the main

---

[2] I still play the sanxian and the yueqin, but my principal focus has been the erhu, the banhu, and the jinghu. My academic career has also led me to acoustical research on orchestration, and eventually cultural acoustics.

[3] I arrived as a Fulbright Scholar and became immediately involved in the music circle. My service to the professional music community in those days included frequent lectures on Chinese music and orchestration. When I arrived at Northwestern, a dozen musician colleagues and I started the "Chinese Music" International Journal devoted to international Chinese music research. "Chinese Music" is today a quarter of a century old and is distributed to 150 countries on five continents.

stream research circle, as most papers written on the subject were simply at rather elementary and superficial levels, and discussions about music outside of the European and American mainstream were consistently shallow.

There were many people I knew who had travelled to China from the U.S. and Europe and who brought back a deep impression of the economic misfortunes of recent China, during the end of the 19th Century into the early 20th Century. Many others were also missionaries who had deep ties to China. Comparatively, this group knew China best. In the sinology community, however, there were little good feeling about the musical art of China. In the Chinese-speaking circles, many were members of the university and research community who moved from China. Most of them did not have very much good feeling about the music of China either. Some of the members of this group enjoyed theatrical music as an entertainment but nothing else. I remember a physicist colleague who told his American friends bluntly that he thought China had no music, but he remembered the operas. I guess the impact of China's recent past had indeed cast a dark shadow over Chinese culture, and Chinese music in particular in relatively recent times.

I, for one, looked at Chinese musical arts and the Chinese musical system from both a scientific and an artistic angle. An anthropology point of view was taken to much of my own questioning. Even when I was a student, I had often wondered what was really happening technologically and musically three millenniums ago, during the Spring and Autumn period, at which time so much of the musical foundations were already laid as we know today. I was interested from an anthropological process angle the events that were important to the development of civilization at that time in this pursuit. It was not until after the completion of some of my own studies of the interaction between the science and technology and the musical arts in those days that I realized, how mankind had gone through such wonderfully exciting periods of development during the Spring & Autumn times, in which the intellectual developmental processes were of the highest caliber and were taking place at incredibly high speeds, when times were good and social environment was conducive. In particular, the very high level of acoustical science which supported the requirements of musical arts of musicians in those days (See e.g. "The Acoustics of Ancient Chinese Bells") is unmatched. Today we are beginning to see perhaps similarly high levels of interaction between sectors in the rapidly transforming United States economy. Will we see another flourishing Spring & Autumn period in the U.S. in the 21st Century?

My work since 1969 is devoted to the subject of "Cultural Acoustics". In Cultural Acoustics we objectively decipher what information in our ears and brains are due to cultural molding and what information is due to actual data received. Musical acoustics as perceived by each person is different - we do not just hear what is played even if we are able to capture all of the sound data that is there. There is always a cultural bias to the data received. What we do hear and process is a product of our own cultural experience as well as cultural upbringing. This phenomenon manifests most clearly when it comes to the question of what chords we hear. For example, musicians trained in Western music often hear minor chords and those related to them when certain Chinese music is played, even when no minor chords are actually present in the music played - in this case the listener's ears are fooled by information overlaid by their own brain on top of the structure of the "shang" and the "zhi" harmonies in Chinese music. In hearing anything related to the "shang" harmony, for instance, a Western musician's brain process automatically adds minor third intervals to the "shang" harmony which contains no minor-thirds. Thus minor chords are perceived because the "shang" harmony appears to have a tonic that is a major second above the major tonic. The *erhu* solo "The Mountain Village Gains New Posture" is a case and point. This favorite solo is without a doubt a happy tune to the Chinese. But to a Western listener it can sound quite minor and even quite sad.

Because of this specialized training in cultural acoustics, I have become a better cultural ambassador today. In fact, my concert audiences tell me these days that they no longer feel I am just a cultural ambassador from China, but rather a person who helps them enjoy all types of music based on cultural acoustics - an interpreter of all music.

I have had many cultural ambassadors before me. Some came to the U.S. and the West for a short time as formal official ambassadors, while some never left China. All of them, however, contributed to this important process of cultural exchange. Mei Lanfang[4] was an early official cultural ambassador. He was sent to the United States by the Chinese government to propagate Peking opera. Most people in the West have since treated his art as <u>the art</u> of Peking opera. During his preparation for the U.S. trip he received expert advice and technical support from such cultural masters in China as Qi Rushan and Liu Tianhua. Qi Rushan was a Chinese elite who had held high positions both in the cultural and political circles. He was so involved personally with Chinese music and Peking opera that he wrote detailed books about musical instruments in Peking streets, and volunteered to provide guidance to Mei Lanfang for Mei's extensive repertoire development. A significant series of dialogue took place between Qi Rushan and Mei Lanfang in the time period before Mei's trip to the U.S. Qi decided for Mei what theatrical numbers needed condensation and what needed emphasis. As a result of this preparation, Mei Lanfang offered a program of Chinese drama "Especially Prepared for American Reception" and "truly representative of the height of the Chinese theater". He included in his repertoire his most famous sword dance in "Farewell My Concubine" and long ribbon dance "The Heavenly Maiden Scattering Flowers." Mei and his troupe would not have had the success they had if it were not

---

[4] Mei Lanfang (1893-1961), Chinese opera performer and one of the superstars of Chinese opera. Mei Lanfang was an extraordinary performer acclaimed for his female roles. Beloved by his fans and respected by his colleagues in the U.S., he was also a noted painter and playwright.

"Farewell My Concubine" featuring Mei Lanfang and the famous painted face Yang Xiaolou

for the efforts of Qi to design the overall trip repertory. The scholarly interaction between Qi and Mei formed the basis for the China-U.S. cultural exchange during the Mei tour. Liu Tianhua, on the other hand, taught Chinese music in the college and university community in Peking. He interacted quite extensively with visiting Westerners in the university circle. When Mei prepared to tour the United States, Liu Tianhua personally notated Mei's music for the American audience. Liu Tianhua provided a complete volume of scores in both Chinese and Western notations (Liu did not travel with Mei). His volume can still be found today at the Library of Congress. In very different ways, Mei Lanfang, Qi Rushan, and Liu Tianhua were all cultural ambassadors of the 20th century in Chinese music.

Mei Lanfang in long ribbon dance
"The Heavenly Maiden Scattering Flowers"

In addition to contributing to the theatrical music part of his art, Mei Lanfang made significant contributions to the propagation of Chinese classical dances in the 20th Century. This work was spurred by the preparation for his U.S. trip. Chinese classical dances were little known to the outside world before Mei's time. For his U.S. trip in 1929-1930, Mei Lanfang consolidated many of the most important elements in classical dances and designed a series of dances for incorporation into his Peking opera program. These included the sword dance in "Farewell My Concubine", long ribbon dances in "The Heavenly Maiden Scattering Flowers", sleeve dance in "Lady Shangyuan", the feather dance in "Lady Xi Shi", the sickle dance in "Lady

Chang E Flies to the Moon", the cup and tray dance in "Magu Wishes the Heavenly Empress Longevity", as well the sword dance in "Hong Xian Steals the Box". His program remains today one of the best and most representative of Chinese classical dance programs. Many others have also contributed to the understanding of Chinese dances, especially from the perspectives of folk dance genres, but Mei Lanfang covered the critical elements and repertoire of the mainstream classical dance movements and artistry. He matched dance design choices with dance and theatrical music in a highly unified fashion, and yet with large artistic diversity. Mei's work is detailed in the volume "Forty Years of Stage Life" (in Chinese), which he wrote with Xu Jichuan and which my father shared with me when it was first published in the 1950s. Other performers of the "dan" female personalities with international and national reputation include Chen Delin, Wang Yaoqing, Cheng Yanqiu, Shang Xiaoyun and others.

In preparing for Mei's trip, Qi Rushan and others spent seven years on publicity and Chinese theater education. In fact their work is still felt today in the West. Whenever Qi entertained international visitors from the United States or Europe, he and his team displayed graphical material for the guests. Whenever dinner was served, Qi would inform them the proper etiquette for eating and tea, and the reasons for the formality. For this many of the visitors have said to be enlightened and grateful. Qi also persistently sent written material to all embassies and students studying abroad. This was how broadly Qi Rushan propagated the Chinese theater. From our point of view today, what Qi did may not have been adequate on the fronts of aesthetics and Chinese musical philosophy. But he and Liu Tianhua and Mei Lanfang were true ambassadors for Peking opera.

■

Theatrical Music & Their Fascinating Vocal Styles

In popular Chinese music today, many compositions have a theatrical music flavor. The reason is simple: the Chinese theater is dramatic, and so is its music. Composers including A Bing[1] have included theatrical passages in their compositions. In the 1970s I had discussed extensively the use of theatrical thematic styles with many composition colleagues from a creative point of view[2]. Liu Wenjin's "Great Wall" has great theatrical passages reminiscent of "Listen to the Pine", also partly theatrical. The theatrical influence here comes in two parts: first in indefinite tightening of rhythm, and secondly in specific vocal style, called "qiang" in Chinese. Chinese theater rely heavily on

---

[1] A Bing is one of the best known composers for the *erhu* and the *pipa* in the 20th Century. He was also a master artist on a large number of classical instruments including percussions.

[2] In the 1960s and the 1970s, there were confusions among Chinese composers regarding the artistic direction of their work. Through the Chinese Music International Network we shared on a periodic basis views regarding inheriting the traditions and creating the new. Personally, the 1970s was the height of my studies in the use of theatrical drama in compositions and I shared the results with many colleagues.

live ensemble accompaniment that is improvised within a well known framework, as a result the ensemble or orchestral music associated with the theatrical performance often have their own instrumental repertoire as well. Today theatrical music is a significant component of all instrumental repertoire.

Opera is an important inter-art form linking the many categories of Chinese musical art. It fuses music, literature, dance, art and other art forms together to create its unique theatrical art, and became an artistic enjoyment integral to all walks of life. The term Chinese Opera (Zhongguo Xiqu) has a very broad meaning. It encompasses all genre of opera that has been created and loved by the Chinese people during the many thousands of years from ancient times to the present. Naturally it also includes the several hundred types of large and small operas popular in the Chinese society today. The wealth and variety of Chinese opera is something difficult to imagine. Take the five coastal provinces in Eastern China (Jiangsu, Zhejiang, Anhui, Fujian, Shandong) for example, there are seventy-seven popular operas. The total number of theatrical operas that are still popular in all regions of China exceeds three hundred. But most of all, the part that the audience loves the most about the music of each, is the vocal style known as the "qiang". The full nomenclature for vocal style is "chang qiang" (singing vocal style). Every regional opera has its vocal style, and every star has his or her own recognized vocal style.

The noted theatrical scholar Ouyang Yuqian remarked in his preface to *Preliminary Collection of Research Material in Chinese Opera* published in 1956 that "the principal difference between Chinese local operas lies in their vocal styles[3]". Based on the major operas today, the four most representative vocal styles are the Yiyang style, the Kun style, Bangzi style (clapper style), and the Pihuang style. All of these stylistic schools have their own long history of development, and they spread far and wide among the masses. They also influence one another extensively. A particular local opera may have a definite vocal-stylistic accent, but often clearly displays signs of influence from other theatrical styles. The four principal vocal styles that we just noted originated in different parts of China, some in the north and some in the south. The Yiyang style was born in Jiangxi province in Central China. It became popular fairly early in the region midstream of the Changjiang (the Yangzi River), Fujian, Guangdong, and the Southwestern region. It invaded Beijing (Peking) during the early Qing period, and dominated the theatrical scene for some time, replacing the gradually declining Kun style. Today almost every major type of opera shows traces of Yiyang style. The music of the Kun style originated in a land of plenty – Kunshan (near Shanghai), where literature and music has had a deep-rooted foundation. It grew under the nourishment of the great team of vocalists, composers, playwrights, instrumentalists including Wei Liangfu, Liang Bolung, Zhang Meigu and others, who absolutely worked their hearts out to perfect theatrical music. It became a theatrical style

---

[3] It is very important to note that all Chinese calls these styles "qiang". Once the "qiang" appears, the musical style is clear. This is sometimes also true in instrumental music as well.

with a very high level of artistic achievement historically. It also gradually became the best-loved theatrical style after mid-Ming. By the end of the nineteenth century, the Bangzi (Qinqiang) and the Pihuang had finally taken over. Like the Yiyang style, Kun opera (Kunqu) has great influence on all sorts of local opera. Some opera types absorb its vocal styles. Some adopt its tunes. Some even perform according to the original Kun script, with very little changes in the music. This is quite different from the situation of the Yiyang style which only left traces of its influence in the opera types. An important reason is probably related to the fact that musical scores were established rather early in the development of Kunqu. The Bangzi style, which includes the famous Qinqiang of Shaanxi Province, has its birthplace in the Gansu, Shaanxi and Shanxi area in Northwest China. Before its inception into the capital, it was already popular all over China, particularly in the North. After the Kun and Yiyang styles which belong to a Lian-qu musical form[4], Qinqiang was the first to appear in a Banqiang form[5]. Even though it was not the creator of the Banqiang form, it promoted

---

[4] Lian-qu musical form consists of joined tunes. This is a popular simple theatrical music form constructed with a series of melodies or tunes. The music of Kunqu (Kun style) and Yiyang style belongs to this category.

[5] In terms of formal design, Banqiang form is another theatrical musical form in Chinese opera. A set of Banqiang music is developed from a single music idea through the expansion, augmentation or diminution of the melody and through changes in the rhythm and speed. The music of a play can be composed with several sets of Banqiang music or only one. Bangzi and Pihuang styles belong to this category.

the musical form, enriched it, and brought it to maturity. Pihuang was born in the region of Hubei and Anhui. In reality, Pihuang was the combined form of two types of music, one of which directly emerged from Qinqiang and is known as Xipi (it is musically of Northern origin), and the other structurally close to the tradition of Qinqiang, but musically and stylistically Southern. They both belong to the Banqiang form, and they formed the so-called Hui-diao in Anhui, and the Hanju in Hubei. The well known Jingju (Peking Opera) in actuality was born of the fine traditions of Kun, Yiyang, and Qinqiang, and based on the Hui-diao[6] of Anhui and the Erhuang and the Xipi[7] of Hubei. Its early form was established during the Daoguang reign (1821-1850), and in the hundreds of years which followed musical celebrities came forth in large numbers. Through their own creations, Peking Opera was developed to today's state of maturity. Naturally, Peking Opera was not the only branch of Pihuang opera. In addition to opera types in the geographical areas of its origin, a large number of operas throughout the Southern provinces are its branches.

As noted above, although each local opera has associated with it a principal vocal style, it frequently has mixed in it other vocal styles. Further, in order to adapt to the likings and dialect

---

[6] The Huidiao are theatrical tunes from Anhui. They became one of the main sources of Peking opera tunes.

[7] Xipi and Erhuang are today the most important modalities in Peking opera melodic progression. Xipi is based in the harmonies of *yu* and *jue*, while Erhuang is based in the harmonies *zhi* and *gong*.

requirements of the geographical area of its popularity, it adds to its basic music all varieties of folk music, tunes and creative compositions. The result is often that the original vocal style became hardly recognizable, and the characteristics of the local opera gradually gained prominence, allowing the opera to mature and to be popularly received. A study of only the four vocal styles mentioned above reveals that the specific combination of accompanying instruments is very different. The original Yiyang style was principally accompanied by percussive instruments. *Di* and *huqin*[8] were added in its local opera branches, but the percussions still perform their characteristic role. The orchestra of the Kun style is the most elaborate among the four vocal styles mentioned and is heavy on winds and strings. Its lead instrument is the alto *di*, other positions in the orchestra being filled by *pipa*, *sanxian*, *sheng*, etc. In some tunes, the *suona*[9] plays the lead with excellent contrasting effects. The name Bangzi style comes from the fact that clappers (bangzi) are used for measures. Other percussions include *luo*, *bo*, *gu*, etc. The most important bowed instrument is *banhu*[10]. Different local Bangzi operas use *banhu* of different range and timbre. Other partners in the orchestra

---

[8] The *di* is the reeded side-blown flute, and the *huqin* is the generic name for all fiddles. They became the first wind and string.

[9] Double reed tunes are a whole different category. The principal double reeds and the *suona* and the high-pitched *haidi*.

[10] The wood fiddle is the best loved bowed string in Clapper operas. The *banhu* is entirely different from the *erhu* family in acoustics. It has a wood plate covered resonator while the *erhu* family has a python skin covered resonator.

consist of plucked strings and *di*. *Suona* is used together with percussions. Bangzi clapper opera music is characterized by its high pitch and intensity. It differs widely from the gentle and moderate Kunqu. As for Pihuang style, we shall use Jingju (Peking Opera) as an example. In Chinese theatrical music, the position of the percussions is traditionally more important than the winds and the strings, except in Kunqu. Take Jingju (Peking Opera) for instance, there are more than ten types of percussions, including all sorts of *luo*, *gu*, *bo* and *ban*, etc. The five key percussions are the *danpigu*, *ban*, *daluo*, *xiaoluo* and *jingbo*. The *danpigu* performer further assumes a conductor role. The coordination between luogu (percussions) performance and voice in Jingju is a highly accomplished art. It is varied and complex. The other half of the orchestra is formed by winds and strings in several combinations. The first group is used for Pihuang styled accompaniments and interludes, and is the most representative. The *jinghu* leads in this group, while *jingerhu*, *yueqin* (four-string moon lute), and *sanxian* (three-string plucked instrument with an unfretted finger board and a python skin covered drum resonator) supports rhythmically and with drum accentuation. In the past hundred years, the performance of *jinghu* has made significant progress in artistic achievements. A number of virtuosos were known. Examples include Mei Yutian, Sun Zuochen of the beginning of the twentieth century, Xu Lanyuan of a later period, and more than ten others. We noted before that an opera often contains several vocal styles. Jingju is no exception. The second combination of instruments, *di* (reeded flute) and *sheng* (mouthorgan), is used for the Kunqu portion of

Jingju. The third combination is a pair of *suona* (double reed). Apart from performance with the percussions, this group does not play with the other groups. Like *jinghu* and *di*, *suona* has its own special qupai tunes, and is an indispensable instrument. Another popular instrument is *haidi* (high-pitched double reed instrument). It performs solo sometimes. It also forms a group with the *di*. Its tunes are mostly borrowed from *suona*.

Opera is an important inter-art form link in Chinese musical art. It fuses music, literature, dance, art and other art forms together to create its unique theatrical art, and became an artistic enjoyment integral to all walks of life. The role of theatrical music in Chinese music is very special. It has its foundation in folk music. It combines voice and instrumental music. The local operas further integrates folk songs, ancient music, vocal styles of all origins, and creative compositions of local artists, each forming a school of theatrical music full of different stylistic variety. The mobility of theatrical groups is fairly high. They not only propagate their own music to other regions, but they also introduce music of other regions to their home. Most importantly, the major and minor operas, despite continual nourishment and change as a result of contacts with other operas, have preserved characteristics and creativity of their own. Therefore the three hundred opera types of China represent an abundant wealth of melodic progression, harmony practice, vocal style and method, orchestration and instrumentation practices for Chinese music.

Jingju has the largest audience among the more than three hundred opera types of China. It was formed during the mid-

Qing period around Beijing. In the beginning of the twentieth century, it propagated from Beijing to the new cultural and economic center of Shanghai and became extremely popular there. Since then, it had spread with the economic power of Shanghai to reach middle-sized and small cities and became a national opera type. Because of its widespread popularity, Jingju has been called by some as "national opera."

In the early pages of Chinese Music, my dear friend Liu Dongbei (Rose Mao), a noted Qing-yi[11], introduced most effectively the artistic know-how for appreciation of the theatrical art of Jingju. Chinese opera is the traditional theatrical art of China. Peking opera in the Chinese language is "Jing-xi". "Jing" means capital. "Xi" is drama. "Jing-xi" is the drama of the capital of China; in this case, Beijing. Jing-xi is translated into English as opera because there are certain similarities, such as song, act, and music, which are the major elements of both western opera and Jing-xi. However, there are many other elements in Chinese opera such as speech, costume, make-up, dance, and acrobatics which are taken into equal consideration. In the western theater, these are presented in separate forms. Peking opera became popular in the last two centuries. The stories played in Chinese opera are deeply concerned with traditional Chinese moral values such as loyalty, kinship, filial piety, trust, peace, and justice. Many themes for Chinese opera, handed down over generations, have become the Chinese people's thinking. The influence is so deep in the heart of Chinese

---

[11] The Qing-yi is the most important female singing role.

people that the knowledge of Chinese opera is one beginning in the adventure of understanding the culture of China.

Those who do not have the background of understanding the Chinese opera will find it difficult to appreciate. Deliberately departing from realism, the Chinese opera uses symbolism to a large extent to convey the events of the story. If a newcomer is provided with a general outline of the theme of the opera, he may have a vague idea of what is taking place. Still, he will not be able to follow the words in the song and speech. What amazes him are the exquisite costumes and the acting, especially the battle scenes with the magnificent acrobats and the most expressive, graceful, and artistic hand and leg movements. Therefore, a brief introduction may be of help to the unfamiliar but curious viewer to understand and be able to appreciate, to some extent, this precious traditional art form of China.

VIRTUAL REALITY

The essence of the Chinese opera is to leave many things to the viewer's imagination. Nothing matters beyond the actors on the stage. Scenery in the usual western sense is not used. The stage is virtually bare. Two chairs and a small table are the basic requirements for the stage. In different positions, they represent a variety of objects. For a judge, the table denotes his chair. For a waitress, the table is her counter. Sometimes a chair is placed on the table. When actors climb onto the table, they are climbing a hill. Several piled-up tables will symbolize a high building, from which a robber may jump down. When a chair is put on its side, it indicates a mound. Four chairs set in a line and covered with a cloth make a bed. Through the art of the performers they project to the audience a mental image of whether the stage stands for a living room, a bedroom, a palace, or a battlefield. The performers use song, speech, gestures, and movements to present the plot to the audience.

A large silk tapestry serves as a boundary between the front stage and the back stage. Performers usually come on the front stage through the left side and leave the stage through the right. Props are used on the stage. They are symbolic. An oar may be a boat or a battleship. A box wrapped with yellow cloth indicates an official seal. When a ball wrapped in a red cloth is thrown on the stage, a man has been beheaded. Floods are presented by small flags painted with fish or surging waves. The weapons are made of wood. The fighters duel fiercely with those weapons, but their weapons never clash.

THE CHARACTERS AND PERSONALITIES

There are several well-defined categories among the roles. These are known as the Sheng, the Dan, the Jing, and the Chou. They represent the male, the female, the painted face, and the clown, respectively. These different types of roles symbolize the characters of certain standardized personalities. Each type of role has its own gestures, way of walking, make-up, costumes, and the particular vocal techniques. The "sheng" are the actors of the chief male roles. This category is subdivided into elderly man with white beard ("lao-sheng"), middle-age man with black beard ("xu-sheng"), young man ("xiao-sheng"), and warrior ("wu-sheng"). Lao-sheng and xu-sheng are men of good quality. The

The vocal style of Ma Lianliang in "Borrowing the Easterly Wind" from "Romance of the Three Kingdoms"

beard may be divided into three parts indicating the righteousness and integrity in the personality. The costumes they wear designate their status.

Lao Sheng actors are required to attain the dignity of bearing and gentle, polished manners of the middle-aged mandarin official or scholar; in military plays they may be a general or high-ranking officer of a gentler and more cultivated disposition than of the painted faces. Their apparel accordingly is of good quality but not too garish in its design or color. A Lao Sheng has a black or white beard, depending on his age, and wears a black hat with two fins on either side which vary in shape according to his rank in a civil role. When a military role is played, the costume is quieter and of a more uniform color than those of the warriors in the painted-face roles, but the armor is also worn. A lao-sheng's voice is gentle, convincing and extremely pleasant to listen to, neither too harsh nor too high pitched, but very firm. Minor officials or land owners who have attained a small degree of responsibility are also included in this role.

Young men's (xiao-sheng) make-up is about the same as the lady's. They use white face powder, rouge, and lipsticks. They appear mainly in romantic love stories. They may portray an army general, but the person in the story is of the romantic nature. "Wu-sheng", the warrior or young men in the army, are

Gai Jiaotian in the role of Wu Song
in "The Happy Forest" from "Outlaws of the Marshes"

specially trained for their fighting roles including much high-level martial art and acrobatic work which demand an extremely high degree of coordination. They usually wear military outfits for different occasions and very little make-up. My favorite Wu-sheng parts were all from the performances of Gai Jiaotian. Gai Jiaotian was China's most celebrated actor of warrior roles. Gai lived through the peak of Peking Opera. He was born 1888 in a peasant family in Hebei Province. Gai was known for his integrity, ignoring the bidding of the abdicated Emperor Xuantong of the Qing dynasty to perform at the imperial wedding. Numerous warlords sought him in vain to celebrate their birthdays or victories. Gai Jiaotian's Wu Song, the famous hero of "Outlaws of the Marshes" was his favorite part. He is known in the Peking Opera circle as the "Living Wu Song". About Gai Jiaotian, Ouyang Yuqian said "His acting is indescribably fine. Whether lively and supple, hard and precise, his movements unfold like a dance. And it is through this acting that his heroic roles, all men of great determination and courage, come to life. He is an artist of great originality, and the audience can always expect some fresh approach from him in every performance. He can be as hard as steel, as flexible as a silk ribbon; swift as a swallow skimming over the water, gentle as the spring breeze in the willows. When he moves, he moves like jewel rolling down a jade platter: his stillness is as immovable as a great rock." Such was the incredible theatrical art of Gai Jiaotian.

The "dan" are the women's roles. "Dan" is also subdivided by age and personality. The "lao-dan" are the elderly dignified women. They appear in their natural complexion and sing with men's voices with a touch of sadness of old age in the tone.

The "Qing-yi" parts lay great emphasis on singing. The performer who plays this part must, before all else, have a first class singing voice. This role portrays the type of faithful wife, filial daughter, elegant queen, or woman of dignity. They symbolize the good and virtuous women as defined in the traditional society of China. Following the old traditions, Chinese women on the stage do not expose any part of the body except their faces and hands.

"Hua-dan" represents women of bold character. They are not women of dignity and high social class. They speak openly, laugh heartily, and often flirt with young men. For this role, a good singing voice is not required but great stress is laid on the acting. The acting is full of charm and seduction, and every moment is full of expression.In the past two hundred years, the part of the "dan" on the stage was played by men. Only in recent years, actresses have begun to take the active role.

Behind a veil of heavy make-up, an actor playing the female character looks just like a charming girl. At the make-up desk, the performer first powders the face with white cosmetics. Then the thin and dark eyebrows are drawn. Around the eyes and over the cheeks are dusted a layer of rose-red rouge. The nose is not touched by red powder, standing out straight and clean. Lipsticks are applied lavishly to curve out a shapely mouth. Eyelashes are darkened.

The "wu-dan" is the young female skillful in fighting and riding. She is beautiful, strong, with feminine charm, and capable of fighting in the battlefield. This role calls for martial art and great acrobatic skills.

"Jing" is the painted face performer. The role of "jing" portrays heroes, warriors, bandits, gods, and supernatural beings. There are nine colors used in Chinese opera for face painting. Each color represents a personality. Generally speaking, red represents loyalty; ochre, honesty; yellow, stubbornness; green, ferociousness; light green, barbarism; blue, fierce looking; black, unrighteousness; white, treachery; and grey, maliciousness. The combination of various colors and designs on the face indicates the complex personality of the role and symbolizes the kind of character in scheming, power fighting, or simply being a bully.

In addition to the make-up, the "jing" wears a padded shoulder jacket beneath the outfit to increase the bulk and very high-soled boots to increase the height. The actor who plays this role must be tall and have a robust voice.

The "chou" is the clown or the comedian. He talks in a joking manner but is not necessarily a fool. He may portray a serious or evil character but hides the true personality with jokes. The task of chou is the same as that of the western clown. He makes the audience laugh in order to break the tension in some serious plays at the right moment.

THE COSTUMES

The costumes are symbolic rather than realistic. They are rich in color and elaborate in design. The style and color indicates the wealth, the official position, and the social class of the roles. Most of the present theatrical costumes have a resemblance to the costumes of the Ming Dynasty (1368-1644) when the people of the high class actually indulged in very splendid robes made of brocade of great extravagance. There are definitively appropriate costumes for every type of character. All ruling class wears long robes and loose sleeves with fancy needlework and bright colors. Servants and low classes wear short jackets and trousers. The officials wear round, black satin hats with a wing on each side. The longer the wings on the sides, the higher is his position. Young men wear long robes embroidered with flowers and birds indicating the leisure type of life style. A general of high rank has four flags attached to his back indicating authority. Officials and generals wear black boots with thick wooden soles. The theatrical armor worn by Chinese theatrical warriors are styled after the steel armor and leather harness worn by Chinese warriors in ancient times. It is made of silk and is very colorful and embroidered. The ladies in Chinese opera wear long gowns and jewelry on their heads. The wealthy ladies wear gowns of bright color and embroidered with definitive designs. A poor lady wears a long gown of silk with very simple jewelry on her head. The phoenix design is used by queens. The dragon design is for the emperors. The flowers and birds are for the young ladies. Chinese written characters, such as "happiness," "longevity", or "fortune" are embroidered on the gown worn by high class middle-age women. The designs used on theatrical costumes now serve as valuable references for fashion experts and those who are interested in oriental fabric designs and fashion.

THE VOCAL STYLE

In Chinese opera, excellence and professionalism are determined by the vocal performance. The mood of singing is expressed by coordinating lyrics to the musical pattern established specifically for it. Singing conforms to set tunes of happiness (Xipi) or a sorrowful mood (Erhuang). Chinese opera lyrics are sung in uniform sentences of from seven to ten words. Every two sentences express one idea. The last word of each sentence must rhyme. A group of four to ten sentences constitutes a paragraph of the opera lyrics. This uniformity was developed from the system of Chinese poetry. The vocal techniques are different for different categories or roles. Middle age (xu-sheng) and old men (lao-sheng) sing in a tenor-like voice. The role of "jing", the forceful man, sings like a baritone. Qing-yi, the modest and virtuous lady, sings in a pure and high-pitched voice similar to soprano. The hua-dan, the flirtatious young girl, sings in a gayly manner. Young men, xiao-sheng, sing in a falsetto to indicate their youth.

Singers are judged by their expressions and whether they execute according to known ban and yan. The ban and yan are terms used for timing. One yan is one beat. Two or four beats make a ban. The singing tempo changes according to the emotions conveyed by the lyrics and the plot.

A Chinese opera actor does not speak his natural dialogue except for the clowns. The clown speaks the "jing bai". "jing bai" means the Pekingese which is the currently used modern Mandarin. The "bai" which is spoken with an unnatural voice, is the stage version of the dialogue used by Chinese people prior to the Qing Dynasty. The leading role in the show begins his or her part in a stage with a long paragraph of "bai", introducing himself or herself to the audience and giving the audience the episode of the show. "Bai" is used also during the course of the play to explain the actions on stage or to converse between the actors.

As early as Song and Yuan, the "zaju" theater was accompanied by strings known collectively as xiansuo. In Beijing opera, the *jinghu* (Peking Opera fiddle) is the principal instrument (referred to as *huqin*) for vocal accompaniment. It is from the silk string fiddle family, has a snake skin covered resonator, and is played with a bow of horsehair. It produces high-pitched tones and uses the largest number of embellishments in performance. In "Deep is the Night" the jinghu performance requires a high level of contrast between straight notes and those with nuances (marked).

and

The leading actors and actresses usually employ their own *jinghu* players. The *erhu* is the "minor" Chinese fiddle, or second fiddle. It is made of red sandal wood and has a python skin covered resonator. It has a lower pitch than the *huqin* and is much softer in tone. It is used as an accompanying fiddle to the *jinghu*.

The *danpigu*[12], or the single-membrane drum, is the lead drum and is very important. The *danpigu* is played by the leader of the orchestra, respectfully called the Drum Master. The Drum Master uses the drum to direct the orchestra and to provide the rhythm of the singing, and to punctuate the acting. The drummer, as the director of the concert, also uses the *ban*, a time beater, to direct the timing of the whole act including singing, acting, and the accompanying music.

The most exciting decorative yet dramatic plucked sounds to contrast with the *jinghu* are from the plucked string instruments the *yueqin*, a lute in the shape of the moon with four strings and *sanxian*, the three stringed fingerboard lute with a python skin-covered drum. The opera *sanxian* is usually played with a bone plectrum or right-hand fingers. They are both used as accompaniment to the *huqin*.

Among the all-important dynamic brass percussion instruments, there are *daluo*, a large gong; *xiaoluo*, a small gong; and *bo*, the small cymbals. Each instrument has its particular purpose. They synchronize the beats perfectly with the action on the stage. They punctuate movements, support the singing, and accent the expression and the gestures of the players.

Acting in Chinese opera is symbolic. Before the performance begins, the audience sees an almost empty stage. A hanging curtain is at the rear. A carpet is on the floor. Two wooden chairs and a small table are usually on the stage. The

---

[12] The *danpigu* and the *ban* are known as the *gu* and the *ban*. They control the pace of each scene, and the transitions between scenes.

interest of the audience is focused on the players who use the symbolic techniques to present the story. The content of the story is then created in the imagination of the audience.

When an actor appears on the stage, he obeys certain procedures in his speech, singing, and movements. This kind of formality must be obeyed throughout the play because the procedures have been worked out and become conventional and by which the audience can be told of what the actor is about to present. For instance, there are no doors or windows on the stage. Instead, two hands together denote the closing of a door which is imaginary. To open a door the actor moves apart his already closed hands. He walks across an imaginary threshold by lifting his foot high and setting it down carefully. As for the long sleeves, there are many symbolic sleeve movements. The sleeves are used to greet, to say farewell, to call attention to other players, to signal to the orchestra to start the music, to clean the dust, to wipe tears, to shade the face in rain, and many others. Standing erect and tense against the outside of an imaginary building shows that the actor is eavesdropping. The lady goes up and down stairs by picking up her skirt with one hand and walking slowly with short steps. Sewing is shown with technically exact movements, despite the complete absence of either thread or needles.

When an actress comes on a stage waving a stick decorated with clusters or tufts of tassels, she is riding on the horse's back. The tufted stick is supposed to be a whip. When she throws the whip on the stage or hands it to a servant, she is alighting. The color of the whip matches with the color of the horse. The player walking between a pair of yellow flags is riding a carriage. The flag is usually embroidered with a wheel outside.

In the case of showing femininity, the actress places her hands at one side of the waist and bends slightly as a curtsey. To indicate the shyness, she raises her right hand, or with a handkerchief, or right sleeve in front of her face. A female character points her finger deftly and glances sideways to show her feminine charms. The way an actress does these techniques indicates the personality she is presenting. A noble lady walks with grace and dignity while a flirtatious woman sways gaily. Between man and woman, there is always a distance. Even man and wife behave with politeness, as they are only acquaintances.

During a fight on the stage, each actor displays his own acrobatic skill. The weapons are not allowed to touch each other. The loser of the battle may roll over on the stage or turn a somersault in the air to indicate defeat. The victor, while not interested in chasing his fleeing foe, will show off some difficult stunts to win applause. A general who has lost his helmet and runs wildly on the stage with his long hair flying loose is supposed to be seriously wounded. The killed fighters fall down on the stage and rise immediately and walk hurriedly off the stage.

THE TRAINING OF CHINESE OPERA PERFORMERS

The movie "Farewell to My Concubine" gives a taste of Chinese opera training. The training of Chinese opera performers is extremely rigid. One has only to see an opera show to realize the long training an actor has to go through before he can present himself on the stage. An early start, usually ten years old, must be made when the actor is growing so he can master the vocal technique with the body movement. The young people who come to the theatrical field have a tough life to go through. They practice the voice by standing in the open air facing a wall in the early morning. They must acquire acrobatic skills. They must also master the complicated leg and arm movements to express the symbolic acting. A successful performer is the one who masters the vocal technique in coordination with various elements such as speech, dance, acrobatics, and symbolic movements.

CLASSICS CAPTURED ON FILM

The cast in the movie "Borrowing the Easterly Wind" was one of the best gathered in my life time. "Borrowing the Easterly Wind" and "A Gathering of Heroes" are two of the best Peking opera movies ever produced in the 20th Century. These episodes from "Romance of the Three Kingdoms" feature Ma Lianliang as Zhuge Liang, Ye Shenglan as Zhou Yu, Yuan Shihai as Cao Chao, Tan Fuying as Lu Shu, Xiao Changhua as Jiang Gan, and Qiu Shengrong as Huang Gai. Each star was the very best in their respective Peking opera roles.

The vocal style is the best part of Chinese theatrical music. Unfortunately most recent performances of Chinese opera in the West have emphasized movement and acrobatics. Regarding high-level mime and virtual reality movements, American audiences are familiar with "Autumn River", a scene from the famous Chinese drama "The Story of a Jade Hairpin". A young Buddhist nun, Chen Miaochang, hastily runs after her lover who is going to the capital for the imperial examination. She meets a kind-hearted old boatman when she reaches a river and entreats him to take her on his boat and help her in her pursuit. Knowing her heart's secret, the humorous boatman teases her, reducing the girl to tears and laughter. Finally, the old boatman, quite sure of his ability, rows and poles the boat with great skill through swift currents and dangerous rapids, thus enabling Chen Miaochang to reach her lover. Throughout the performance, no boat is shown, but the audience is sure that both performers were on a boat, which turns and turns.

■

What Makes Chinese Music Chinese?

My grandfather Chen Chang-tai was a *xiao* player. The *xiao* is the ancient end-blown flute quite important in the Shanghai area. His favorite pieces included the "Three Six" (Sanliu), which at the time was called "Meihua Sannong". His contemporary Xia Bao-sheng perfected the Tanci version of the "Three Six", now known as "Tanci Sanliu". As many of you know, the "Three Six" is a class of composition like the "Xing Jie" (Processional) popular as instrumental and ensemble pieces since the Yuan period. Therefore there has been numerous versions, all of which do not sound the same. In fact, throughout China, such extensions, contractions, and embellishments are popularly used as composition techniques. Tanci is the famed ballad singing of Suzhou, one of the most scenic cities of China not far from Shanghai (the other is Hangzhou). "Tanci Sanliu" is derived from the version of "Three Six" popular as Tanci music. In the 1960s Gu Guanren made "Tanci Sanliu" extremely popular among orchestras as a plucked string ensemble favorite.

Instrumental music in China is typically non-programmatic, as "Three Six" is. They are pure instrumental music. China was the first civilization in which pure instrumentals were important art forms, and in fact China was the only place pure instrumental music existed until quite recently when Western classical music became written strictly for instruments. The emergence of pure instrumental music in China can be attributed to several factors. First of all, the musical interest of instrumental music was recognized extremely early in China among early civilizations because of the existence of silk strings. On these fabulous material used as strings on the acoustical resonators of Chinese instruments, the musicians discovered the vastly different acoustics of stopped tones and harmonics. This phenomenological observation combined with mathematical developments and acoustical developments produced the first generation of musicians anywhere equipped with musical acoustical preferences for the sound of instruments, and in particular, the love for use of contrast between the earth, heaven, and human tones - respectively open strings, harmonics, and stopped tones. During this very process the art and science of temperaments developed quickly, making China the most advanced civilization in this most fundamental area of musical systematics. Secondly philosophical development in China integrated music into the mainstream of the frontier of scholarly activities very early in China. Instrumental music was recognized as one of the highest form of interaction between humans and the universe.

UNIVERSAL RESONANCE

Musicians in Shang-Zhou China particularly enjoyed their musical resonance with the universe. This was possible because silk string instruments were mature, and the centuries of acoustical studies took place on their silk string instruments.

China is the first country in the world to raise silk worms and to weave silk fabrics. As a result China is also the first civilization to have a complete range of string instruments. In 1958, in the most important archeological find in silk history, scientists discovered spun silk fabric, silk belts and silk thread woven from home-grown silkworms in the lower layer of the Neolithic remains at Qianshanyang, Wuxing[1] in Zhejiang Province. Tests date these fabrics to 4,700 years ago. My family in Wuxing has been in the silk trade and the silk business for numerous generations and my father is a pioneer in international silk and brocade trade in the 20th Century. Silk is the important material that formed the basis for ancient trades which developed into the Silk Routes on land as well the oceanic Silk Route. Silk is the first industry in human history where the highest quality control was possible in the making of strings for musical instruments. I used silk strings on my earliest *erhu* fiddles. On resonators employing silk strings, Shang-Zhou Chinese gained incredible insights into the importance of the acoustical properties of the string. The most developed form of Chinese chamber music today is the Silk & Bamboo, and the Chinese Music Society of North America is today internationally known for its Silk & Bamboo Ensemble. This art form of eastern China has many relatives up and down the coast of China and in inland regions. The large area of Wu (Jiangsu Province) and Yue

---

[1] Wuxing County is located on Lake Taihu. This region has therefore been historically known as Huzhou, the Lake District.

(Zhejiang Province)[2] is the home of Silk & Bamboo, and the people of Shanghai all came from Jiangsu and Zhejiang and neighboring areas. This is why sometimes Silk & Bamboo has been referred to as being from Shanghai.

The *qin* is a very personal instrument for personal musical enjoyment, while the *qin* and the *se* form a pair in private music making and friendship among scholars and members of the literary community. On the *qin* resonator, Shang-Zhou Chinese gained incredible insights into the importance of the acoustical properties of the string. Throughout human history, the study of the string has been a much larger subject than the study of the wind. The reason is simple. Strings, especially those with high material quality control, offer the most elegant acoustical system for the study of overtones. It was on silk strings that the Chinese musical masters mastered their understanding of string harmonics, and the offers of a performance system in which stopped string is contrasted with open string and harmonics. Because the *qin* is such a personal instrument, early *qin* players listened and heard all of the subtle differences between tones generated by different performance techniques and tones generated by different parts of the instrument's acoustical spectrum available to the player. The other instrument on which our forefathers communicated with the universe with was the *xiao*, end-blown flute. The *qin* and the *xiao* were scholar's instruments for communication with their

---

[2] Wu and Yue were the most important ancient kingdoms in these regions. The Emperor Gou Jian, for example, was Emperor of Yue, and the famous beauty Lady Xi Shi of Yue was herself from the Taihu lake region.

inner sanctum and the universe. For this critical function, the *qin* and the *xiao* are intentionally not instruments with a huge dynamic range, unlike the *suona*, the *zheng*, or the *di*[3]. Those other instruments were for an audience, and thus require a large dynamic range.

The *qin* (pronounced "chin") is a Chinese plucked string instrument with elongated trapezoidal and slightly arched wooden box resonator and seven strings but no bridges. The strings are plucked by the right-hand fingers while the left hand fingers stops the strings at desired lengths. Thirteen small ivory or mother-of-pearl disks inlaid in the resonator surface provide reference for the stopping points and positions of harmonics. Over two-hundred notations are used to indicate the playing technique, stopping position, and tonal requirements. The use of harmonics in melodic progression is a characteristic feature of compositions. A total of ninety-one choices is available. The open strings, the stopped pitches and the harmonics are used in contrast with each other. A very large repertory exists for this instrument and best known players include Si Kuang, Si Wen, Si Xiang (Spring and Autumn and the Warring States Period, 770 BC - 221 BC), Cai Wen-ji (177 AD -?, Han Period), Ji Kang (227 - 263 AD, Jin Period), Guo Chu-wang (1190 - 1260, Song Period, Wang Yan-qing (1866 - 1921), Guan Pinghu (1887 - 1967), Xu Yuanbai (1893 - 1957), Zha Fuxi (1895 - 1976), Wu Jinglue (1906-) and others. Recent masters who cover many schools include Gong Yi.

---

[3] The master Ji Kang made specific comparisons with these instruments.

The body of the *qin* consists of head, body, and end parts. The ancients considered the *qin* to have head, waist, and back. They went as far as calling these parts the golden boy head, the jade maiden waist, and the fairy back. Its various components are also named in terms of the dragon, the phoenix, gold, and jade. The ancients designed the *qin* to be 3 feet 6 inches and 5 minutes in Chinese lengths. It signified that one revolution in heaven was three hundred and sixty five degrees and a year consisted of three hundred and sixty five days. The *qin* has upper and lower surfaces, connoting the interaction of heaven and earth. There are thirteen "*hui*" markings for performing harmonics, signifying the twelve months in a year plus a leap-year month.

There is systematic difference between the *qin* and most other string instruments of the world. Most string instruments such as the violin use a narrow area for fingering (such as the fingerboard of the violin). The *qin* uses its complete surface for fingering. Most string instruments have pegs (for tuning strings) located on the upper left. The *qin* has all pegs located at the lower right. Apart from the *konghou* (harp) which has severe shape restriction, all string instruments have lowest string located near the player's body. All strings on the *qin* have the same length, producing no shape restriction for the *qin*. The *qin* however has lowest string located on the outer side, with respect to the player. Many string instruments have sound holes on the front surface, and the *qin* has sound holes on the back.

The *qin* master Zha Fu-xi once said that "some music historians tend to consider string instruments of the Asia-Europe continent to be of one origin because most string instruments are of similar constructions. But the case of the *qin* is opposite to all common construction of string instruments. Does it have a different origin on the banks of the Yangzi and the Yellow Rivers which possibly had its own ancient system of musical culture? Recent discoveries in Chu culture illuminate this point. The *qin* today appear to be connected to the Chu and Han string family. Xu Shen's interpretation of the form of *qin* in ideograph appears incorrect".

The *qin* and the *se* are popular string instruments of ancient China. The *se* has movable bridges and the *qin* has none. Their number of strings also varies quite a bit from period to period and from region to region. Both instruments were frequent musical partners for a long time in history. The musical treasures of Zenghou Yi in Hubei, for example, contain many such string instruments in the orchestras (see e.g. Lee, in *Chinese Music*, several issues in 1979). The seven string version of the *qin* now used was popular during the Han period more than two thousand years ago. *Qin* artists including Shi Zhong, Zhao Ding, Long De and others were known in history. It was also absorbed into the royal court. The famous *qin* artist Ji Kang lived at the end of the Han period. One of the earliest *qin* score has been handed down by a folk artist Qiu Ming (500-590).

Chinese artists who played the *qin* during the Six Dynasties period expanded upon the repertoire of the Chu and Han culture. When the Tang period came, great artists such as Zhao Ye-li, Dong Ting-lan, Chen Kang-shi and others assimilated other music including the Zhu school of music (Zhu-jia Sheng) and the Shen school of music (Shen-jia Sheng), boldly created large numbers of compositions and theoretical treaties. Unfortunately due to the shortsightedness of the elite class to follow, much of this treasure was lost.

In the weak Song period, many scholars still played the *qin*, but good compositions were few (See Zhongguo Yinyuejia Xiehui, 1960). From historical documents remaining, we know of *qin* artists including Sun Dao-zi and Zeng Yi-hai. The scholar Fan Zhong-yan is known to play the *qin* well. Ouyang Xiu frequently discussed the aesthetics of the *qin*. Su Dong-po not only played the *qin*, but also composed. He recognized that *qin* music "was the sound of Zheng and Wei", meaning it came from folk music. Two small compositions of this period "Gu Yuan" and "Huangying Yin" can not be compared to compositions before Song. But at the time that Song was defeated, numerous *qin* artists emerged with great artistry and social outlook. Guo Chu-wang of this time period who lived from the Song to the Yuan period composed the masterpiece "Xiao Xiang Shui-yun" (Mist Over the Xiao and Xiang Rivers). Mao Ming-zhong composed the colorful masterpiece "Qiao Ge" which had its origin in Chu music. Wang Da-you composed for Wen Tian-xiang in jail the suite of "Ju You". They are such tremendous compositions that they are passed down to us.

Metering of Chinese music is difficult. Western musicians who study silk and bamboo music today are often fooled by the metering indicated by the simplified published scores. When studied in detail, the performances bear no resemblance to these scores. And here I am not referring to the oversimplification of the score as to the pitches performed and the lack of notations for embellishments. The worst situation is encountered when the scores lied - the accentuations do not fall where they are supposed to be according to western conventions, i.e. the strong beat did not occur at the beginning of the bar. In actual fact, Chinese music is best not metered. Phrasing and breathing marks do work, however. In fact these are so much more honest and reliable if you pay attention only to them, and pay no attention to the bars. Traditional Chinese musicians don't look at the bars.

Chinese classical music is timeless. The rhythmic elements and tempo are considered the last items of importance, in order not to constrain performance. This concept made classical Chinese compositions easily adaptable to changes in musical taste of rhythm amd metering, which are strong functions of time period. The result is the successful propagation of a large number of the best compositions through time, making them therefore truly timeless.

While scores are written by musicians of instrumental and vocal music, the rhythmic elements and tempo are considered the last items of importance, in order not to constrain performance. This concept made classical Chinese compositions timeless and easily adaptable to changes in musical taste, which as we now well know is a strong function of time and period. The result is the successful propagation of compositions through time, making them therefore truly timeless. This is the case of the instrumental school of the *qin* and the vocal school of the *qin-ge* (the *qin* songs). The horizontal zither *qin* is an important historical instrument and has associated with it a very large number of known compositions passed down through history. Its methods of notation is based on the concept of timeless music. Yet at the same time the *true character* of the music and the player, as in the requirements of changes in tonal quality, is very much emphasized throughout.

Music that is truly timeless has been the dream of composers throughout the ages. In this paper we discuss the rhythmic philosophy - a timeless philosophy - that exists in Chinese classical music. The metering of Chinese music is difficult and we will discuss why that is the case. While scores are written down by musicians for both instrumental and vocal music, the rhythmic elements and tempo are considered the last items of importance, in order not to constrain performance. This concept made classical compositions timeless and easily adaptable to changes in musical taste, which is a strong function of time, as a result of which these compositions are passed on successfully through time, and are therefore truly timeless. We analyze the changes in that philosophy during different periods, and the recent neglect of it in the 20th century.

The breadth of rhythmic concepts is often a focus of attention during concerts, pre-concerts, as well as post-concert discussions during the tours of the Silk & Bamboo Ensemble and the Chinese Classical Orchestra in the 1970s, the 1980s and the 1990s. Compared with popular music or classical music in the United States, the musical performance at concert programs of the above groups has been said to offer "an astonishing range of rhythmic variations" by critics who are usually comparing the performance they just experienced with other performances that they are familiar with, usually Western classical or popular. The basis of the comparison is a musical experience truly engaging and fascinating. To look at the comparison closely, however, one may encounter the age-old questions of "What really makes interesting music?" and "How do we compose successful music?" Were those both practical as well as philosophical questions on the minds of the great Chinese classical composers? I imagine they were to a limited extent. But apparently more on their mind was the question of where we fit as a human race in the grand scheme of the universe, and in space and in time. Those thoughts led to the way Chinese classical music was written and the way they were passed on as we've come to know them now.

TRANSCENDING SPACE AND TIME

That was certainly the case for a long time, before the Song period. Music of Tang (618-907) and before was distinctly different from music afterwards due to one very important point: the perspectives of the musician and the composer. Ancient music through the Tang period was *cosmic* in perspective. Celestial bodies and their relation to earth and to humans occupy a large part of the experience of man's very own existence among the cosmos. Man's coexistence with natural forces formed a large part of where musicians thought they stood. The study of musical acoustics flourished. After Tang, however, man became different, and significantly more concerned about his immediate human environment, and his own individual thoughts. Was there an advancement or a decline in the philosophy of life? We can probably look at it two ways. The music before Tang and through the powerful part of Tang (Tang established global political and military power and remained powerful until towards the end) gave a sense of destiny and pride, in terms of understanding of the position of the human race, where civilization really fitted, where it could make the most contribution universally, and where the highest interests of life could be found - e.g. in the mathematical and acoustical arena of sound and music. In the music after Tang we found musicians not only to return to the description of ancient sufferings that occupy everyday life, but also to amplify the emotions and thoughts associated with personal problems and social problems. Music reflects social progress and social change; The entrance of the Song period (960-1279) is thus the beginning of a politically weak period in Chinese history, globally speaking. Philosophy and aesthetics deteriorated in this time period, and so did music. Folk music, however, flourished in the silk and bamboo school and in the reed and percussion school, focusing more on acoustical effects of the ensembles, a new accomplishment that was more independent of the content of the titles of music.

Many westerner scholars and musicians who studied Chinese music at the turn of the 20th century encountered a large number of problems in transcribing Chinese music. A frequent problem was of course associated with the "embellishments" and the "nuances", that varied distinctly from performer to performer, and from one performance environment to another. Strictly speaking, these situations were not to be called "performances" because despite the fact that audience existed the players "played", and allowed their emotional priorities to take charge as they "jammed" for their own musical benefit and thus "did not perform" with the intention of satisfying their audience's musical expectations. Then came the larger problem of reading the scores. So frequently western scholars and researchers were astonished to find no tempo or meter was indicated. During performances, complex patterns of pitch and interval usage and instrumental acoustics were apparent but were going too fast for a proper digestion (Yang, 1984). *Qin* students who studied the *qin* scores faced the same problem (In fact many researchers would settle for interpreted scores with timing and rhythm written in, see e.g. Xihu Qinshe, 1993). Much confusion was attributed to difficulties with cadences but little attention was paid to the true cause of the problem: a different perspective with respect to the "Rhythmic Philosophy" that is present in Chinese classical music.

This can be understood today by looking at how music changes with time, and, in fact, the possible thinking of the Chinese masters, who notated their music as scores, in deciding what to put down and what not to put down, in order to make good music immortal and allow the creative process to be forever present whenever music is made.

Let us look at the evolution of music throughout the ages. Several types of changes reflected in the change of times. The sound, the instrumentation, whether we liked reedy sounds, whether we liked dynamically contrasting sounds, and whether we liked more subtle musical flow contributes to one area of musical psychology. The main area of change through the ages could be found, however, in rhythm and meter. A song, or an instrumental piece, at different times in history would acquire different rhythmic treatment. But the main musical material, the interval contrast in the melody and the harmony, would remind us that the same piece of music is being played. The Chinese masters caught this concept and used it to the fullest extent.

The interpretation of *qin* music is an art that makes music timeless. Pitches, intervals, and important changes in tones are all specified, but no meter or rhythm is usually stated to constrain the player. This was the case for a long time until more recent scores such as Wang Yanqing's scores from Shandong which had such constrains.

The concepts here refer to the "timelessness" of classical compositions. Look at "The Orchid in Seclusion" (Youlan) which has been interpreted countless number of times by today's artists. Looking at some versions (See Zhongguo Yishu Yanjiuyuan Yinyue Yanjiushuo and Beijing Guqin Society, 1982, Zhongguo Yishu Yanjiuyuan Yinyue Yanjiushuo and Beijing Guqin Society, 1983, and Zhongyang Yinyue Xueyuan Zhongguo Yinyue Yanjiushuo and Beijing Guqin Society, 1963) from Guan Pinghu, Wu Zhengping, Xu Lisun, and Yao Bingyan, they have each recreated a rendition based on preferred tempo and rhythmic preferences at the time of the recreation.

When Kong Zi, Confucius, traveled to all the main principalities in China and found himself not seriously considered by any, thoughts began to emerge. On his way back to the principality of Lu, today's Shandong Province, he found the fragrant orchid among weeds, and found himself in similar situations. He sang on the *qin* these thoughts. According to what we know today, there are more than thirty versions of this music, all instrumental without word. Some contained a single movement, some three, some eight, and some more than ten.

Today's popular music overemphasizes pulses and beats, to such an extent that many young musicians will have trouble with a piece of music when they can not clearly sense the pulses and the beats. But in actual fact, in the current overemphasis of pulses and beats, sensitivity towards metering and time is totally lost. Only well known and popular accentuation patterns are kept, and many new age composers are therefore trapped.

Bear in mind what we are talking about here is performance and composition as the creative processes of music making. When we become uncreative in any one aspect of what music really is, we are in deep trouble. That is the problem with a lot of the commercial music today.

In Chinese music, the allocation of time and apportioning of space is decided by the amount of thinking involved and the appropriate distribution of weight.

The weight in terms of length in time and forcefulness in dynamics are measured according to the performers' perception and not according to that of the composer. This is best illustrated by such pieces as "Listen to the pine", "Wedding Processional", and many others.

We hear nowadays frequently recordings by music school graduates in China who could only go by the score, and the recordings of these pieces are absolutely terrible in the sense that no music or genuine interest could be found in the performance.

Many music critics who heard these recordings have told me that these recordings sounded like background music or studies.

When true artists like the Shanghai Traditional Orchestra of the 1950s played "Wedding Processional", the musical interest was immeasurable, primarily because true music came out of the creative and collaborative music making process of musicians who ignored the "standards" of the score.

Thanks to efforts by *qin* masters at clubs such as the West Lake Qin Society, the horizontal zither *qin* is becoming a popular instrument again today. It is an important musician's instrument and historical instrument, and has associated with it a very large number of known compositions. Its methods of notation provide food for thought on the subject of timeless music. The method of notation of *qin* music has been widely studied. In particular, the manner in which master players recreate (the recreation process is known as *dapu*) the music according to their interpretation of the score (*pu*) reflects significantly the manner in which the Chinese people treat music. The tempo and speed in which a composition is played upon *dapu* interpretation can vary drastically between master players, yet everyone knows the same piece is being played when they listen to the different renditions. This phenomenon offers spheres of expanded thoughts for composers today.

Frequently in western music, we find musicians paying a lot of attention to the score, sometimes with so much attention that the creativity of the music making process is overlooked. As we all know, preference for tempo and rhythm are strong functions of time period. Putting too much emphasis on these aspects of a music can seriously impede musical development. I will illustrate why this is the case. When Whitney Houston sings a song that had earlier been sung by Dolly Parton, the rhythmic element of the song is totally modified. The new rhythmic modification gives the song a totally new life, and yet it is really the same song sung in a different style, and in this case reflecting preferences of this new time period. Such adaptation processes do not occur as frequently in classical music today. The *dapu* process of musical thinking for the *qin* offer new dimensions for advancements in classical music composition. The *qin* masters over the ages wrote their pieces anticipating changes in rhythmic and other preferences in music making, thus making their music new and lively at all times, in turn making their music timeless.

This philosophy, however, is not well understood by many Chinese musicians, who have not been exposed to true Chinese music, today. As a result of miscommunication and misunderstanding, *qin* music has been looked upon only with historical relevance and little musical enthusiasm, in many cases.

Timeless music has been a unique and profound philosophy of the Chinese musicians. Unfortunately, timelessness has not been on the mind of the music community in recent decades. It has been neglected. Late nineteenth century and early twentieth century Chinese music was in one of the poorest shapes in Chinese history. Little effort on the part of the Chinese society was put into music. During the war years of the Sino-Japanese war, vocal and choral music were composed for important reasons, and they played a most positive role in increasing the will of the Chinese people in the war. Music as a whole was economically and socially revived after 1949 and professional musicianship became supported at a very high level by the Chinese government. The timelessness philosophy of Chinese music was, however, not recognized nor studied in the music schools, except perhaps on an individual basis. Much of the success in this recent period centered on the collection of folk music, and the revival of folk traditions. On the professional performance front, the composition and arrangements of this period were not entirely healthy. Following the west, rhythm and tempo became the more important elements. The Chinese, during this period, started almost from scratch philosophically. Substantial effort was put in to "modernize" and follow the blip in western music's historical development of emphasizing the importance of atonal compositions. These efforts of "tide riding" proved unfruitful. Today, we have produced a large number of music students who are skilled in western composition styles, and western aesthetics in orchestration and acoustics, but have paid little attention to their own "timeless" musical philosophy. This is similar to the neglect of the generalized "harmony" philosophy in (see e.g. Shen, 1991) Chinese classical music - music schools went after specialized but restricted harmonic concepts from the west and dumped the larger generalized harmonic framework of Chinese music.

The purpose of our discussion here is to alert the music community both in China and in the west that: (1) the music that we hear on a day to day basis in China is possibly not very Chinese or even unique any more, (2) it is time that China and the world look seriously at the "timeless" perspective of musical composition which was for a very long time a powerful tradition that sustained music development, in the only civilization that prospered in music without interruptions despite drastic political changes domestically and globally.

CHINESE MUSIC & CULTURAL ACOUSTICS

Chinese music is built on a totally consistent harmonic system which controls melodic progression, orchestration, and temperament use. It is perhaps the only major musical system in the world that has such all-encompassing requirements on all aspects of its music, and at the same time allowing the largest flexibility in the acceptance of harmonic intervals into music. In the 1960s and the early 1970s through the work of the Chinese Music Society of North America, we discovered the cyclical harmonic skeletons known as *zhi, shang, yu, jue, gong* in the Chinese harmonic system. Before this work, those terms were for a long time referred to as scale steps. This set of harmonic skeletons is self generating, always in tune without equalizing temperaments because its system does not believe in the twelve tones alone. The same harmonic intervals which are the basis of the Chinese harmonic system were found to appear prominently in the design of the overtone structure of the ancient dual-pitched bronze *zhong* bells (see Shen, 1987). The same harmonic intervals are completely utilized in the design of Chinese silk and bamboo musical instruments, and in particular, is the basis for string tuning on the *qin*, the *sanxian*, the *zheng*, the *pipa*, the *erhu*, the *tuoyin erhu*, the *matouqin*, the *zhuihu*, the *jinghu*, the *banhu*, the *liuqin*, and the *ruan* family. This I believe I first discussed in 1976 at the First Chinese Music International Conference held at Northwestern University in Chicago. Towards the end of the 1970s, something more profound took place in our research. For the complete system of Chinese musical instruments, we discovered an intimate relationship between the overtone structure of musical instruments selected by the Chinese musical system and the harmonic preferences of the Chinese system. In retrospect it should have been obvious that this was the case. As soon as the Zenghou Yi bells were discovered, we launched a massive project looking into the acoustics of ancient Chinese bronze bells. In that project we were able to, in great detail, separate the musical bells from the non-musical bells. We studied complete overtone structure of all existing Shang and Zhou bells and was delighted to find the acoustical design of bells of each period, and in particular in the case of the *zhong* musical bells established direct connection between the choice of their overtone structure and the Chinese harmonic system as we know it today. Acoustics is thus a cultural thing, in addition to being a physical thing!

Acoustics is part of physics, but what music research and music appreciation need is Cultural Acoustics. In physics, octaves and fifths are harmonic, while in cultural acoustics, thirds and seconds can be. The preference of these artistic harmony is in the realm of culture. The similarities and differences between the musical aesthetics of each cultural system is also based on Cultural Acoustics.

The cultural acoustics of a musical system determines the preference for musical intervals and instrumental overtone spectrum. It further determines what temperaments and orchestral culture the system will support. These considerations are the foundation for all music theory and for relationships between all cultural entities. Regarding the preference for orchestral fundamental spectrum in the Chinese orchestra, I have written extensively on the shengguan and the tanbo spectra and their use in Chinese classical music.

The concept of melody is quite different in Chinese music, compared to what is generally accepted in the west. And the various ideas about melody we've come to know in the west simply do not apply to Chinese music. There are enormous number of implied notes in Chinese music that do not need to appear in the score. This is conceptually similar to the unspecified tempo and metering in *qin* music, so as not to constrain performance creativity - a score should not constrain the performer, a score is used to pass on information about a composition, and "people" (the performing artists) will "create" music in a performance. This is paramount in Chinese music and is an incredibly important concept. In order to understand the artistic pathways of Chinese music one must understand the philosophy of Chinese music. Chinese classical music does not pretend to specify the specific length of individual notes, tempo, or what is known as rhythm - the reason is one transcending space and time. We must recognize that the above-mentioned interpretive tools such as tempo and rhythm are functions of time. Different periods throughout history had their own preferences on methods of musical interpretation. Once the score is fixed, and fixed in too much detail, the composition "will not live" forever. Why not do according to the requirements of the time and regional preference in the "dapu" creative process. The dapu process, well-known all over China, is the creative process of recreating a music for performance using tips from a "framework" score. Melody in a composition in Chinese music is also in a similar situation - every period and every region has preferences on the expansion of complexity and number of decorative notes versus decrease in the number of notes (what is usually known as embellishments). If we were to force every note to be written down, the music would have lost its artistic life entirely.

Modern western music is played primarily according to scores, although in avant-garde music composers are trying very hard to move away from fixed performances. Orchestral scores are written so that every nuance is specified, and conceptually all notes are part of a melody. As a result of this training, when western orchestral musicians hear a performance of the "Old Six Measures" by Chinese masters and begin to examine its Gongchi score, they are shocked: "The score is so simple - how come the performance is so rich and complex?" At this time we must point out that "Chinese acoustical space includes implied musical notes - It includes a creative cultural acoustics!" The source of this is in generalized harmonic theory; whether actually performed or not, harmonic notes or notes in the same artistic system "are heard" by the brain. This is the essence of cultural acoustics. The musical art of Chinese music is deep in its intrinsic thoughts. Its beauty is also in the acoustical and artistic manifestation of these thoughts.

REFERENCES

Lee Yuan-Yuan, in *Chinese Music*, **2**, numerous issues (1979).

Lee, Yuan-Yuan and Shen Sin-yan, *Chinese Musical Instruments*, Chinese Music Society of North America, Chicago (1999).

Shen, Sinyan, Acoustics of Ancient Chinese Bells, *Scientific American*, **256**, 94 (1987).

Shen, Sin-yan, *Chinese Music and Orchestration: A Primer on Principles and Practice*, Chinese Music Society of North America, Chicago (1991).

Xihu Qinshe (West Lake Qin Society), *Xu Yuanbai Danchen Yibai Zhounian Jinianche* (100th Anniversary of Xu Yuanbai's Birth, in Chinese), Xihu Qinshe, Hangzhou (1993).

Yang Yin-liu, A Bewildered Western Musician, *Chinese Music*, **7**, 4 (1984).

Zhongguo Yinyuejia Xiehui (All China Musician's Association), *Yinyue Jianshe Wenji* (Collection of Essays on Musical Construction, in Chinese), Music Press, Beijing (1960).

Zhongguo Yishu Yanjiuyuan (Chinese Academy of the Arts) Yinyue Yanjiushuo (Music Research Institute) and Beijing Guqin Society, *Guqin Quji* (Collection of Guqin Music, in Chinese), People's Music Press, Beijing (1982).

Zhongguo Yishu Yanjiuyuan (Chinese Academy of the Arts) Yinyue Yanjiushuo (Music Research Institute) and Beijing Guqin Society, *Guqin Quji* (Collection of Guqin Music, in Chinese), Vol. 2, People's Music Press, Beijing (1983).

Zhongyang Yinyue Xueyuan (Central Conservatory of Music) Zhongguo Yinyue Yanjiushuo (Chinese Music Research Institute) and Beijing Guqin Society, *Guqin Jicheng* (Anthology of Guqin Music, in Chinese), Vol. 1, First Half, Zhonghua Press, Beijing (1963).

■

My Concise History of Chinese Musical Instruments

Over the years I have gained significant insights into the incredible way in which musical instruments of the world have emerged and became popular. The system of Chinese musical instruments is a family of musical instruments utilizing all available acoustical material and resonators. In fact the name reserved for musical instruments is "qin", or resonator. The history of Chinese musical instruments has been a history of new resonator discovery, new use of physiology in acoustical excitation, and musical acoustics. Acoustical research in the 20th Century revealed a most distinguished history of the science of music in China. Ancient China possessed a level of acoustical science that was essential in supporting the elaborate musical art of those periods. Physics and engineering worked hand in hand to perfect musical instruments and to arrive at desirable orchestration. Coupled acoustical systems were invented in every period. New performing methods were found in all regions. Throughout the ages preference for musical instruments have changed greatly. Very early instruments naturally emphasized wind and percussion. Globular flutes *xun* and end-blown flutes *xiao*[1] first appeared in China 8,000 years ago. Panpipes *yue* and mouthorgans *he* were invented very early. The early invention of silk strings formed the basis of the design of string instruments. The bronze age brought about the fabulous dual-pitched Chinese musical bells.

Incredible as it may seem, just about all instrumental groups were complete before Qin. During the early dynasties of the Shang (16th-11th Century BC) and the Zhou (16th Century-221 BC) periods, sophisticated silk-stringed musical instruments were used which were not to be carried when played (unlike the later lutes and fiddles which are portable) and they were all quite large - these were the times of *qin*, *se*, *zheng*, and the horizontal *konghou*[2]. These major instruments remain today, with the bass instrument the *se* becoming completely unpopular nowadays. The *se* is a bass string instrument. It works extremely well with the *qin* in a duet, and as bass instrument in an orchestra. The *se* is traditionally divided into two parts - top and bottom - when played, thus utilizing both hands in contrapuntal melodies at the same time. (The *se* is still one of the best bass

---

1 The oldest known vertical flutes were the *gudi*, the bone flutes. The oldest group of end-blown *gudi* is 8,000 years old found in Neolithic sites at Jiahu in Wuyang County of Henan (See Shen, 1991), and these Wuyang *gudi* contained the complete interval preferences of the Chinese people. But today *xiao* is the name given to end-blown flutes.

2 The *konghou* is the harp. Old *konghou*'s were horizontal, like the *qin*, and the *se*. The more popular *konghou* is vertical, and it became popular in the Han period. The konghou is used today as an accompaniment and orchestral instrument.

instruments for the Chinese orchestra, but because of the modern love for bowed strings it's been shelved.) At a later time the bowed *yazheng* appeared to become popular, especially in Sui times. The *qin* utilized contrasts between harmonics, stopped strings, and open strings as major categories of tone quality in composition. The *se* was frequently used in *qin* and *se* duets - thus a fingerboard instrument is contrasted and supported by a bridged instrument. These instruments and the *zheng* were plucked, and the *yazheng* bowed. The resonator used here can be classified as a long box which amplifies notes made on strings which transmit their energy via ridges, posts or bridges. The one instrument which is uncommon after those periods was the *zhu*, on which a stick-bow was bounced on strings. On arts depicting *zhu* performance, e.g. in the Mawangdui relics, the *zhu* was played like a cello with the bow bouncing on its strings. The discovery of the musical treasure of Zenghou Yi from the 5th Century BC provided examples of two orchestras: one based on jin-shi-si-zhu (metal-stone-silk-bamboo) and another based on si-zhu (silk & bamboo). The large court orchestra was dynamic in volume and symphonic in acoustical impact, utilizing a large bell chime (a single musical bell is a *zhong* and a bell chime is called a *bianzhong*) which would occupy the complete stage of a chamber music recital hall today, and a large stone chime (a single musical stone is a *qing*, and a stone chime is a *bianqing*). This large orchestra utilized various mouthorgans in the categories of *yu* and *sheng* (the *yu* is a melodic instrument and the *sheng* is a harmonizing instrument, both in the free-reed mouthorgan category), the *yue* (panpipe) and the *chi* (the *chi* and the *di* are side-blown flutes[3]) and a large number of silk instruments such as the ones we already described above. There were the "Shi" Music Officers assigned to various lead instruments including the *zhong*, the *qing*, the *sheng*, the *yue*, the *bo* (ceremonial bell) and other musical instruments.

The next period of expansion in Chinese instrumental music was the Qin (221-207 BC) and the Han (206 BC-220 AD) period. The portable lutes were a hit. During the Qin-Han period, many hand-carried and portable instruments became widely poplar. These included the *ruan*, *pipa*, *qinhanzi*, *hulei*, and others, which can best be classified in the lute family - but because of their performing technique, they really were vertical members of the "tantiao" family of China (see Shen, 1981 and Shen, 1991), the horizontal members of this family being the *qin*, the *zheng*, the *se* and the *yangqin*. One form or another of all of these instruments are in use today - thus this period is extremely important for Chinese instruments. Today three general groups of the vertical tantiao family are popularly known: (A) the *sanxian* group which uses drum resonators covered with skin membrane on two sides, coupled to a fingerboard neck. Members include the large *sanxian* and the small *sanxian*, (B) the *ruan* group which uses disc-like resonator coupled to fretted neck. Members include the *ruan*, the *yueqin*, and the *qinqin*, and (C) the *pipa* group which uses pear-shaped resonator with convex back, with frets. Members include the *pipa*, and the *liuqin*.

---

[3] Most ancient cultures had a number of end-blown flutes. China was the inventor of the side-blown flute, or transverse flute.

New tone colors were favored from the Wei-Jin through the Tang, when double reeds, new percussions and fiddles were the new sounds. The Wei (220-265) and Jin (265-420) periods up to Tang (618-907) saw the complete disappearance of the bell chimes and the stone chimes. In fact, the dual-pitch design of the musical bells and the performance techniques were completely lost until the 20th Century[4]. Many portable percussion instruments were popular. These include the *bo* cymbal, the *paiban* for keeping tempo and orchestral direction. The *fangxiang* xylophone[5] was popular and completely replaced bell chimes and stone chimes. The Sui-Tang period fancied the use of double reeds. In particular the cylindrical double-reeded *bili* became a popular sound, together with the *jiegu* drum performed with two sticks. The famous Xuanzong Emperor of Tang composed several dozen musical numbers featuring the *jiegu* as solo instrument and the whole musical scene became very exciting with the popularity of various double reeds and

---

[4] In 1978, after the Zenghou Yi musical treasures were unearthed, the Chinese Music Society of North America launched a comprehensive project on the study of the acoustics and performing techniques of the bianzhong, as part of our ongoing Chinese Harmony Project which comprehensively investigated (a) interval building blocks, (b) temperaments, (c) overtones of instruments, (d) tuning of instruments, (e) performance art of instruments, and (f) composition and orchestration, as one unified subject. During this project, the mystery regarding the design of the dual-pitch system on the zhong and the performing methods of the bianzhong was completely solved.

[5]At a later time, the *fangxiang* xylophone would be almost completely replaced by the *yunluo* gong chime, which is still popular in the 20th Century.

percussion instruments from western China. The Sui-Tang courts were one of the biggest on number of musical staff. There were permanent installations of orchestras from more than ten different regions of China in the Tang courts. In addition to the *bili* as a double reed, the conical *suona* was popular.

Also during the Sui-Tang period the age of true fiddling began. This was a time when bowed strings were officially imperial instruments. The Chinese fiddles are true fiddles in that they were intended to be bowed when invented and not converted from lutes. The *xiqin* fiddle of the Sui-Tang period, which used a long bamboo stick as its bow with no horsehair, became the predecessor of the present-day *banhu* fiddle. Then during the time of Genghis Khan various types of the Mongolian *matouqin* horse-head fiddle became known more widely to the majority of the non-Mongolian Chinese. This fiddle utilized a horse-haired bow. A cross-fertilization of fiddles then took place all across China and its vicinities. From this point on all fiddle players of China became exposed to bows with horse hair, and utilized it until the present time. This practice also influenced lute players and instrument makers in Europe who adopted the concept of the horse-haired bow for bowed lutes that would be used as new string instruments.

From the Song period, which was creatively incredibly weak, to the present, we saw the rising popularity of the fiddles. The Song (960-1279), the Yuan (1271-1368), the Ming (1368-1644) and the Qing (1644-1911) periods saw the consistent popularity of the fingerboard lute *sanxian*, which had been important in theatrical music and ballad singing during this time.

In the Ming period, the great musician Wei Liangfu was a master of the fiddle *tiqin*. He used this fiddle as a main accompanying instrument for Kunqu singing and in the silk and bamboo ensemble. Compared with the *xiansuo* string music of the north, according to Li Yu of the Qing period, the *tiqin* was more crisp in tone. It's a long fiddle that used no *qianjin* (Thus the whole length of the strings were used) and bowed with horse-haired bow. The *tiqin* was popular before the *huqin*, and was later replaced by the *huqin*. Of course, the *huqin* family remains extremely popular today. Thus from Sui-Tang to the present time, we saw several developments pertaining to the fingerboard that are prevalent: (1) the popularity of plucked instruments with no frets, as well as (2) the popularity of bowed fiddles with and without a fingerboard[6]. Very few new resonators were introduced after the Sui-Tang period. The last dynasty-the Qing period was a time when the Qing court was very interested in reviving ancient instruments such as the *bianzhong* to ascertain a main-stream Chinese status. However, the Qing court failed miserably - they were able to construct only modest-quality ceremonial bells but not musical bells at all. As a result, many scholars in China and abroad during the Qing and the Republic period were also terribly confused about what was a *bianzhong*

---

6 The more regional *zhuihu, zhuiqin, leiqin* fiddles all use fingerboards, whereas the highly popular *erhu, zhonghu, banhu, jinghu* fiddles use stopped free strings with no fingerboard - a drastically different concept when it comes to left hand performance techniques, compared with fingerboard instruments.

or how it was played. It showed a serious lack of understanding of Chinese musical culture during Qing times.

The 20th Century saw the elevation of many ensemble and orchestral instruments to a solo status. In particular, the second fiddle, already popular in its orchestral role because of the statistics of use in regional ensembles and orchestras, became the most popular solo instrument in ensemble and orchestral works. A disheartening phenomenon in the 20th Century is the collapse of the motive forces behind regional instrumental practices, as a handful of "professional" composers try to simplify the orchestral scene in larger cities. They composed for a simplified Chinese orchestra which lost all of the musical interests and cultural acoustics of Chinese orchestras. They lost track of Chinese aesthetics, and most importantly, they lost track of the principles behind the acoustical space of the Chinese orchestra. Thus it is a matter of education, and a matter of the mind set.

The regions and provinces of China are drastically different culturally. The cultural acoustics of the music in each of them are individually unique, and yet all Chinese. The reason is that the Chinese were different peoples. The culture of the people are so different that a person from a neighboring province may or may not understand what he hears in this province. Over the thousands of years the Chinese people are unified by a single language and a single Harmony System. As a result we have the most interesting situation of the coexistence of many Chinese orchestras, each having its cultural acoustical specialties, and yet all are unified by the Chinese Harmony System. It is thus a mistake to take apart the regional Chinese orchestras and try to produce a single Chinese orchestra, because they are already unified through the Harmony System. But it is highly desirable to broadly present the different ways of doing things instrumentally in these different regions and provinces, so that their cultural acoustics and musical interests can be further propagated and, most importantly, utilized in new compositions.

REFERENCES

Lee, Yuan-Yuan and Shen Sin-yan, *Chinese Musical Instruments*, Chinese Music Society of North America, Chicago (1999).

Shen, Sin-yan, The Tantiao (Pipa) Strings, *Chinese Music*, **4**/1, 3 (1981).

Shen, Sinyan, Acoustics of Ancient Chinese Bells, *Scientific American*, 256, 94 (1987).

Shen, Sin-yan, *Chinese Music and Orchestration: A Primer on Principles and Practice*, Chinese Music Society of North America, Chicago (1991).

■

The Music of the Chinese Orchestras

When the Shanghai Traditional Orchestra played "Wedding Processional" in the 1950s, the musical interest was so immeasurable, primarily because true music came out of the creative and collaborative music making process of musicians who ignored the "standards" of the score. Such creative improvisation is the norm for orchestral performance. The Chinese orchestras have the most diversified tone qualities and frequency ranges. Different orchestras belonging to different geographical regions and culture have vastly different preferences on the range of instruments. They also present an amazingly large spectrum of colorful instrumental practices. Broadly speaking, the instrumental makeup of Chinese orchestras can be divided into plucked strings, bowed strings, percussions, and winds. During the 1960s through the 1970s I investigated, analyzed and studied the orchestration practices which were important to the makeup of the many, purely instrumental and theatrical orchestras of China, to prepare us for the optimized usage of past experience in Chinese composition and orchestration. Geographical and cultural barriers have often prevented the true appreciation of music from different stylistic schools of China and the proper interpretation of music as performed by orchestras not familiar enough with the stylistic origin of a regional music. My investigation aimed at providing better insight into the interpretation of the many schools of orchestral music and the composition of orchestral music.

The Sizhu orchestras (silk & bamboo) such as the ones playing the "Processional" and the Chuida orchestras (reed & percussion) form the largest groups. The silk and bamboo orchestras and the reed and percussion orchestras practice rather different orchestrations. "Si" here refers to plucked and bowed strings, and "Zhu" refers to the bamboo reeded winds. The Jiangnan Sizhu orchestra, one of the most popular Sizhu orchestras which originated in Eastern China, uses a wide range of plucked strings including the *pipa, yueqin,* small *sanxian, zheng, yangqin,* and *qinqin* (or a *zhongruan*). The best example of its acoustics can be found in recordings of "Processional" (Xing Jie). These plucked strings fall into several distinct categories as far as performance techniques and tone qualities go. The *zheng* and the *yangqin* are open-stringed instruments (for the range and tuning of the principal plucked strings, refer to Lee Yuan-yuan [Lee, 1979]). The *zheng* is performed with fingernails and the *yangqin* is performed with a pair of "Zhu" (bamboo hammers). The *pipa, yueqin, qinqin, ruan* and *sanxian* belong to the "Tantiao" system. Their performance techniques are based heavily on the fundamental action of "Tan," playing with the index finger to the left or downward, the "Tiao," plucking the string with the thumb upward or to the right. *Sanxian* differs from the rest of the members of the "Tantiao" family, especially in left-hand techniques. It is not a fretted plucked string and a different variety of manipulation of the tone is possible on the *sanxian*. The plucked strings have a long history of ensemble cooperation. Let us look at the traditional partnership of *pipa* and *sanxian* in more recent times. Take "Tanci" for example. "Tanci" of the Jiangsu province is a well-known style of music in which recitative singing is accompanied by instruments. In the Qing dynasty, the principle instruments used in "Tanci" was already *sanxian* and *pipa*, with the occasional addition of *yangqin*. Today, when only one instrument is used, it is most likely the *sanxian*. When two instruments are used, the traditional partners *sanxian* and *pipa* are played by a male performer and a female performer respectively, the upper part of the melody being performed on the *sanxian* (small *sanxian*) and the lower part on the *pipa*. In a joint venture of "Hui Shu," several *pipa*'s, several *sanxian*'s, the *qinqin* and the *erhu* are used.

As performers of orchestral music will tell you, the correct blending of even two instruments takes many years and decades of experimentation. Because of the improvisation nature of instrumental ensembles, the orchestral structure of all of the orchestras of China are based on long-time partnership of the instruments. Partners since the 16th century used in "Kunqu," including the di, *xiao, sheng, pipa, guan, sanxian* and so on, probably have the greatest influence on the Sizhu orchestras.

The Chuida orchestras vary widely in composition. Various sizes and types of *suona* (double reed conical wind) and *guan* (cylindrical reed pipe) are the lead instruments in many of the Chuida orchestras. Sunan Chuida orchestra of Southern Jiangsu, however, emphasizes more on the *di*. The pitch characteristics of the percussions varies drastically from one orchestra to another. But within one orchestra, only very narrow pitch variations for any one percussive instrument is allowed. Otherwise the percussions simply do not blend correctly and unwanted effects may result.

Today popular instruments such as *pipa, ruan, zheng, erhu, zhonghu, dahu* (or *gehu*), *dihu* (or *beigehu*), *di, sheng, suona, houguan,* etc. have been consistently absorbed into orchestras which were originally more localized. One example is the Yuju (Henan Bangzi) orchestra which originally consisted of *piaohu* (*Yuju banhu,* alto-ranged), *erhu, sanxian, sheng, di, luo, gu, cha, bangzi* etc. is now expanded to include all of the above instruments (Liu, 1979) which are popular all over China. The trend of the local orchestras is definitely towards expansion in instrumentation.

The flourishing of regional music-drama which continued through the centuries since the Song dynasty (960-1279) until the present day has created a large number of theatrical orchestras. Musically, they vary tremendously in style and instrumentation. The Yue opera (Yueju) orchestra, Pingju orchestra, Peking opera (Jingju) orchestra, etc. belong to this category. Bowed strings, the *huqin*s, play very important roles in their orchestration. We will analyze their music at a later stage. The Liyuan Opera orchestra, however, does not use bowed-strings as the lead instrument.

The Liyuan Opera orchestra of Fujian is a highly sophisticated orchestra in Southern China. Its principal instrumentation employs *dongxiao* (vertical flute) as the key wind and *pipa* as the key plucked-string. The string, wind, and percussion division is as follows:

String: *pipa, sanxian, zhonghu* (or large *erhu*)

Wind: *dongxiao, pinxiao (di), da-ai* (large *suona*), *xiao-ai* (small *suona*)

Percussion: *tanggu, paigu* (small drum), *dapai, xiao pai, guban* (four pieces of pillow-shaped wood), *daluo, xiaoluo* (medium *tangluo*), *wanluo* (bowl-*gong*, or small *tangluo*), *xiaojiao* (also known as *goujiao*, another small *tangluo*) *gubianluo, niuzhan, liangzhan* (also known as *shuangyin*, larger than *niuzhan*, the pair of *zhan*s are brought to contact when played), *shuangling, dabo, xiaobo, du.*

Among the wind instrument, *dongxiao* and *di* are seldom used together, the reason being incompatibility in tone quality. The percussion section is led by the *tanggu*, unlike the case of Peking opera where the *danpigu* (small high-pitched single-membrane drum) leads the percussions. The *paigu* (small drum) in the Liyuan Opera orchestra is only used when the music tenses up. We note here that the geometry of the *paigu* is closer to the small drums used by Kunqu orchestras and Yiyang styled orchestras. The inner diameter of the membrane is larger than that used by Peking Opera orchestras. The performance of the *tanggu* is complemented by the *xiaoluo* (the medium *tangluo*, as in puppet theaters of Southern Fujian). The rhythmic pattern and dynamic effect of the *tanggu, xiaoluo* and *paigu* performance suggest a close relation between Liyuan Opera music and the Yiyang style. Like in a number of other popular theatrical music, the ending phrase of a melodic section is often divided into two parts sung in harmony (Huadong, 1955).

THE ART OF STRING INSTRUMENTATION

The Chinese tradition of using strings in the orchestra is quite different from practices of the European or the American tradition. In a large majority of instrumental orchestras, as opposed to the theatrical orchestras, the plucked strings have assumed a leading role in orchestration over the bowed strings, for the very reason that the Chinese plucked strings have such a long standing history of popularity, and musical development.

The theatrical orchestras, which became popular during the last five hundred years or so, often employ a lead bowed-string. Excellent examples are the *erhu* in Huju, *jinghu* in Peking opera, alto *banhu* in Yuju, *banhu* in Qinqiang, *zhuihu* in Quju, *zhonghu* in Yueju, *touxian* in Chaoju, and so on. Qi Rushan made a very interesting observation (Qi, 1949): In Peking opera, the *yueqin* traditionally played an extremely important part. When the *jinghu* performed a long and extended note, the *yueqin* would always take over with its lunzhi, creating a dramatic orchestrational effect. For some reason, the *yueqin* was later de-emphasized and its performance was so deteriorated that only one string of the *yueqin* was used anymore in Peking opera, and the fingernail techniques were replaced by one of plectrum. It was probably a result of both the over-emphasis of bowed strings, and the shrinkage of theatrical orchestras due to economic decline. In any case, the Chinese experience indicates that the plucked strings are at least as important as the bowed strings in an orchestra, if not more important. There is a slight tendency these day of a decline in the ability to use plucked strings in their well-experienced roles. But more experienced composers seldom fall into that trap.

Statistically speaking, *sanxian* is probably the most utilized instrument of the many types of orchestras of China. *Sanxian* differs from other members of the plucked string family in that it is an instrument utilizing the resonance of a skin membrane whereas *pipa, liuqin, ruan, yangqin, zheng, yueqin* and so on utilize the resonance of a wooden sounding board. *Sanxian* probably have the longest history of popularity among the masses compared with the other plucked strings. The small *sanxian* of Jiangnan has a small drum (drum is the name by which *sanxian's* python skin-covered resonator is known. It may be related to the fact that the resonator is acoustically a drum, and the ancestor of *sanxian* as a drum, *xiantao*) and its characteristic tonal quality is that generated by a string under relatively high tension over a resonator covered with a thin skin, sometimes percussive. The combined effect of the string and the small drum is rich in higher harmonics and its performance is highly ornamental, a typical example being offered by the beginning section of "The Past and the Present" (Jin Xi) performed by the Shanghai Minzu Yuetuan (Shanghai Traditional Orchestra). The effect of tonal manipulation of the small *sanxian* arouses musical interest of an unpredictable kind. *Sanxian* is a fretless instrument. The characteristic gliding embellishments on some of the model distinguished notes creates immense overtones which form an important contribution to orchestral effects. In "The Past and the Present" for the reeded flute and the orchestra the *sanxian* is critical in its orchestrational effect. Effects of small *sanxian* of the distinctly Jiangnan or other Southern character can also be found in such outstanding orchestra work of the silk and bamboo school as "Wedding Processional" (Xing Jie), "Zhonghua Liuban" (the moderately embellished orchestral version of Lao Liuban, Lai, 1979) performed by the Shanghai Traditional Orchestra (China Record M-032). The musical role played by the large *sanxian* in the Chinese orchestra is very different from that of the small *sanxian*. Its tonal quality is one that gives a feeling of a string-membrane coupled system with the string under low tension. It has a large drum almost 9 inches along the long axis and offers a full and deep voice. A dynamic performance on the large *sanxian* can be heard in "Days of Emancipation" (Fanshen De Rizi) performed by the Xinying Traditional Orchestra.

The roles of the small and the large *sanxian* are really quite different: the small is acoustically manipulative and thus arouses excitement, and the large has low and stable voices and long reverberation. These effects thus make them both important in orchestration.

The *Yangqin* is known as the most indispensable plucked string and one of the most indispensable of all orchestral instruments. in Jiangnan Sizhu and Guangdong music (Cantonese music) carries the most intricately ornamented melody and ascertains the harmonic bases of the music. To get a feeling of the kind of sophisticated musical performance we are talking about, one may listen to "Wedding Processional". The octave doubling harmonically important is know as "chen yin", and they are critical in the resulting acoustical effect. The performance is highly improvisational; The player reacts to the environment in which he or she plays, in particular to whom he or she is playing with. The degree of ornamentation is a function of time and place and ensemble partner.

The popular "Rain Falls on the Plantains" (Yu Da Bajiao) is a good example of the Guangdong styled role of *yangqin*. The orchestrational effect of *yangqin* in Jiangnan Sizhu and Cantonese music are similar in many respects, with the *yangqin* in "Rain Falls on the Plantains".

The versatility in the performing techniques of *yangqin*, employing a large number of combinations of wrist and finger actions, and the wide frequency range of four to five octaves, makes *yangqin* an indispensable member of the Chinese orchestra. The noted conductor, Zhen Xun, of the Zhong-Guang (Central Broadcasting) Traditional Orchestra once remarked that the *yangqin* and the *sheng* are so important to Chinese orchestration that one must have them before one has anything else. That statement is really not an exaggeration. The hammers of *yangqin* are a pair of specially designed bamboo strikers whose hammering surfaces are covered with thin leather. The performance of the *yangqin* can be controlled so that within a passage, certain notes can be made muffed and others crisp and bright. This type of orchestral performance can be found in the first movement from "Fishing Song of the East China Sea" by Ma Shenglong and Gu Guanren, performed by the Shanghai Traditional Orchestra with the maestro He Wu-qi conducting.

THE ART OF REEDED WIND INSTRUMENTATION

A name for the *sheng* documented 15th century BC on oracle bones was *"he"*, or "harmony". The use of *sheng* in the orchestra is a practice at least three thousand years old, and indeed the coupled vibration of the pipe and free reed has the effect of blending, or harmonizing other instruments whose overtone structure present obvious tonal gaps. In the northern styled orchestras, where double-reeds such as *haidi*, *suona* and *guan* are the key instruments, the *sheng* is an indispensable accompanying instrument. The Jiangnan styled orchestras have had a long history employing the *sheng* for harmonizing the plucked strings, the bowed strings and other bamboo winds.

The harmonies performed on the *sheng* is designed so that the differences in volume among the members of a chord is utilized to characterize the tonality of the music. The deliberate doubling of important notes is frequently used. On the other hand, the same principle of loudness contrast is also used to build chords which perform the function of special effects, sometimes disharmonizing. The *sheng* is not just an accompanying instrument, or one that produces only special effects. Its transparent and sweet voice, when used to play Chinese harmonies, produces a mellow and full sound. The *sheng* in solo passages creates a distinctly Chinese atmosphere. The *sheng* is used in "the ocean at dawn" in *sanban* (free tempo), from "Fishing Song of the East China Sea" by Ma Shenglong and Gu Guanren as performed by the Shanghai Traditional Orchestra. A phrase on the *zhongyin sheng* (middle-register *sheng*) is contrasted with a phrase of identical structure with a pitch center an octave higher on the *gaoyinsheng* (high-register *sheng*). This practice creates both register and tonal contrasts, and is often done. "The Dance of Yao" (Liu Tie-shan, Mao Yuan and Peng Xiuwen) features a *sheng* dance solo passage, accompanied by a duet of *di's*. In this dance the combined effect of the *sheng* and the *di's*, providing higher harmonics simulates the south-western styled *lusheng* performance. However, it is important that the volume of the *di's* does not overshadow the *sheng*.

The number of sounding pipes, called miao, in the *sheng* has gone through many changes during the course of history. The ancient *yu* for instance, had over thirty miao's (mostly thirty six). The Jiangnan styled *sheng*, also known as *Susheng*, have seventeen miao's. In today's traditional orchestras, the number of miao's has returned to about thirty six (Fang, 1978).

The Chinese double-reeds offer a complete continuum in frequency range and tonal quality. The popular *haidi's* have A_4 or B_4 as their fundamental tone and span a compass of two octaves all the way into B_6. The *suona's* occupy a complete range of fundamental tones of G_4 to A_2, with a high of G_6. The *haidi's* and *suona's* are near-conical resonators, and their low register range is joined both in pitch and in tonal quality of the large diameter *guan's* which are straight cylinders, forming the bass group of the double-reed family, with another group of *houguan's*, which are small diameter straight cylinders with a horn, covering the common range of the medium register. The popular *houguan's* have fundamental pitches ranging from G_3 to A_2, and the large *guan's* have fundamental tones from G_4 to G_3 (three popular ones have compasses G_4-A_6, D_4-E_6, and G_3-C_6).

The geometrical construction of the double-reeds, as schematically shown below, makes use of several acoustic properties of pipes. First, the highest of the group, the *haidi's* and the *suona's* are conical. As we know, for the same length of pipe, a perfect cone has a fundamental tone an octave higher than the straight cylinder. Then the *houguan's* are small cylinders with a horn which tends to raise its lower frequencies, thus filling the middle continuum. The bass range are ideally occupied by the large straight cylinders, *guan's*.

This double-reed family from cones to cylinders forms an integral part of the Chinese orchestra in its chuida wing. The "Overture" (Xu Qu) of the dance drama "The Dagger Society" (Xiao Dao Hui) composed by Shang Yi and performed by the Shanghai Opera's Traditional Orchestra uses the bass *guan* (*di-guan*) for its powerful beginning passage:

In the middle register between A_2 and E_5, if the shrill tone of the cones (*suona's*) is not desired, one switches to *houguan*. For example, "The Dance of Yao" uses an F-*houguan*. The traditional performance of these double-reeds offer tremendous tonal interest in their embellishments and offer qualities important to the intensity and warmth of the orchestral effect.

THE ORCHESTRA'S TONAL SPECTRUM AND ITS ARTISTIC UTILIZATION

I gave a series of Orchestra Lectures in China in the 1980s where I discussed the makeup of the fundamental tonal spectrum of the Chinese orchestra from both an acoustical as well as an artistic angle. Many of our conclusions support the traditional use of tonal components in the regional and historical Chinese orchestras. We further explored the role of the interval in the musical language of China, and the role of natural intervals as standards for the acoustical space of musical compositions. The inspiration for the contents of this lecture series comes from all existing compositions, old and new. I therefore thank all of our composers throughout history. A summary of the findings are included here.

The acoustical makeup of the Chinese orchestra can be analyzed in terms of fundamental tonal spectrum groups. Compared with the Western symphony which has one fundamental spectrum group - the violin group - the Chinese orchestra has two fundamental spectrum groups - that of the sheng-guan (reeded winds dominated by free reeds) and that of the tan-bo (plucked strings). The acoustical space of the Chinese orchestra is thus richer than that of the Western symphony. The roles of the special color instruments, in particular the erhu vertical fiddle and the percussions, must be mastered for all composers.

There are several dozen major Chinese orchestras now known. They differ in orchestration methods and in artistic techniques. To the musicians of today and the modern musical stage, the paramount question has been the intelligent utilization of several hundred instruments in the chui (reeded winds), da (percussions), tan (plucked strings), and la (bowed strings) categories of performance technique. How do we maximize their power together and how do we maximize the level of artistic sensitivity that compositions utilizing them can provide.

Concerning the orchestration emphasis of the regional orchestras, I have touched upon in my series of papers on the foundation of the Chinese orchestra published in Chinese Music. Each one of those orchestras can be recognized as a prototype for extensive practical utilization. In this paper we do not restrict ourselves to any one geographical region. We will study from the angle of orchestra acoustics, we will study the acceptance to the audience of orchestral art, and we will discuss and deduce the appropriate composition mentality for writing orchestral work.

The first concept I will discuss is the fundamental tonal spectrum of an orchestra. An orchestra is vastly different from an instrument. An instrument has a frequency spectrum, representing a distinctive range of tone. Some instruments have tones of a similar type throughout its range. For example, the violin and the *liuqin* both have a wide compass and the tonal quality of each does change from the high register, through the middle register, to the low register, but the basic tone quality throughout the compass is of the same type. The same is true of the *banhu*, another instrument based on wood plate vibration as the violin and the *liuqin*. Other instruments such as the *erhu* or the saxophone are quite different from the group we just discussed in that they project a vastly different personality at different ranges: the tonal quality at different register are of different types. To the instrumental composer, both types of instruments are easy to grasp. But when it comes to orchestration the situation is vastly different.

The symphony is a more recent product of mankind. Its orchestral spectrum is quite a bit simpler than that of the Chinese orchestra and is therefore better understood. It utilizes a basic tonal spectrum of the violin family. All other instrumental spectra present are not fundamental to the orchestra's orchestration and are supplementary. These other spectra are used for special color and function in contrast with the fundamental spectrum of the violin family. The sound of the symphony orchestra when it comes through our perception is that of the violin group.

The Chinese orchestra also has both types of spectra, fundamental versus supplementary. But because of the extraordinarily extensive period of practice, the Chinese orchestra possesses an extraordinary range of resonators and acoustical materials. Its fundamental tone thus can have several possibilities. Broadly speaking, the Chinese orchestra has two groups of fundamental tones, and the Western symphony has one.

Many of our twentieth century compositions for the Chinese orchestra mistakenly used the huqin vertical fiddle group as the fundamental spectra. This is contrary to acoustical understanding. We have witnessed in practice that when the 'huqin group' is used as the fundamental spectrum for composition, its power is rather limited, and the benefit cost ratio is low.

What makes a fundament spectrum and what makes a special color spectrum are decided by the intimate relation between the spectral characteristics and the musical psychology of the audience. For some instruments, solo use is more powerful standing against a fundamental orchestral spectrum, but when used in group the tone becomes muddy. Other spectrum can be extremely powerful, easily controlled in spectral width, and highly flexible in texture. This is particularly true of the tan-bo (tanbo) - plucked string family, the sheng-guan (shengguan) - reeded wind family of China and the violin family of Europe.

What is the foundation of the fundamental tones of the Chinese orchestra in terms of acoustics and musical psychology?

FIRST FUNDAMENTAL SPECTRUM - THE SHENGGUAN

Probably the most important but often unnoticed group is the shengguanyue. This group has the incredible ability to grow and shrink in tonal breadth, and can be easily utilized for fundamental orchestral spectrum. Here the two terms 'sheng' and 'guan' represent a full range of coupled resonators: free reeds and air-column in resonators, membrane and air-column in resonators, and pressured reeds and air-column in resonators. By itself the shengguanyue is a complete orchestra - it possesses all the quality to make an orchestra. This quality can only be judged with acoustical and musical psychology standards. The nomenclature used here departs from the traditional use of the term shengguan. Shengguanyue is used to represent the most important tonal spectrum - the shengguan spectrum of the Chinese orchestra. This spectrum consists of

- the shrill tone of the pressured small reed,
- the full-bodied tone of the coupled air-column, and
- the full harmonies from the resonance of free-reed and air-column.

Decades ago the Chinese music community became enthralled with the tonal capabilities of the *lusheng*[1] orchestra of Southwestern China. The musical interest offered by the *lusheng* orchestra is but a subset of the musical interest of the shengguan group. But from the interest in the *lusheng* orchestra one can imagine the power of the shengguan spectrum.

The high, middle and low register *sheng*s (free-reed mouth organs) and the *bawu* (free-reed flute) provided rounded smooth tones characteristic of free reeds coupled to air columns. Here the *bawu* utilizes a single reed at different angles for coupling to a large range of air columns. As a result the dynamic range systematically decreases towards the high notes. This must be taken into account when the *bawu* is used in the orchestra. The combination of the sheng and pressured reeds (the *sheng* and the *guan*, the *sheng* and the *suona* and the *haidi*, for example)

[1] The *lusheng* is a fascinating group of mouthorgans from Southwestern China with naturally amplifying air columns. They come in all sizes and the total range is so comprehensive that the lusheng orchestra is capable of playing the complete range of tone colors of a string orchestra. It is thus a synthesizing orchestra, if viewed from acoustical vantage points.

has been used in a large number of traditional orchestral experiences. The low-register *houguan* (bass double-reed cylindrical air-column) comes in handy for low-range support. The combination of the *xiao* (end-blown flute), the *gaoyinsheng* (high register *sheng*), the *zhongyinsheng* (mid register *sheng*), the high *houguan* and the low *houguan* form an incredibly expressive spectrum (see next page).

It should be pointed out that the shengguan group is often torn apart today in compositions. Loud combinations of *suona*, when unsupported by the *di* (reeded flute) and the *sheng* group, are monotonous. This technique can be utilized when the balance of dynamics is fully realized in the dynamics space of the composition envisioned by the composer.

Unstable membrane and air column make up the tone of the *di*, which moistens the high frequencies of the pressured reed. In my work I found this method very useful. Solo *di* passages, and *di* duets in thirds and fourths heard frequently in recent decades are not effective. Traditional use of the *sheng* and *di* combination has its acoustical reasons.

SECOND FUNDAMENTAL SPECTRUM - THE TANBO

The second fundamental Chinese orchestral spectrum is tanboyue, or plucked strings. It is well known that the plucked string orchestra of China is the most complete in the world. It is complete in several ways, but most importantly in the compliments of resonator types, acoustical material and performance techniques. The resonator types and acoustical

Also present are the harmonic effects of the *zheng* and the *yangqin.* The percussions used here include the *ling* bells, the *bangzi* clapper, the large *dabo* cymbal, the low *luo* gong, the flower-vase *dagu* drum, and the *bianzhong* bell chime.

materials used are not haphazard, but have been developed for orchestral group use over the centuries. On top of that, performance techniques most highly developed allow a vast number of tone patterns to be used by composers of the plucked-string orchestra music. As a result the plucked string orchestral group possesses the powerful capabilities of tonal contrast, dynamic contrast and textural contrast.

What we are discussing here is the function of plucked strings as a fundamental tonal spectrum for the orchestra. This is a much broader use in concept than what is represented by the plucked string ensemble used in pieces like "Three Six" or "The Camel Bells." In those compositions the plucked strings were treated almost strictly as individual tones to be exploited and as components of a multi-part harmony. Those are simplistic uses. One should look at the breadth of the harmonic content in this fundamental spectrum and treat it as an orchestral texture capable of growing and shrinking.

Let us examine what makes this group so versatile. This branch of the Chinese orchestra is unusually rich in tonal quality. It encompasses:

- high-frequency range plate resonators excited by tantiao plucked performance,

- low-frequency range plate resonator excited by tantiao plucked performance,

- middle to low frequency range membrane resonator excited by tantiao plucked performance,

- broad frequency range plate/box resonator excited by jixuan struck performance,
- low range long resonator/long string open-string excitation, and
- low and broad range long resonator/long string fingerboard excitation.

The extent of spectral versatility of this component is no less than that of the shengguanyue. The combination and organic utilization of both groups are unmatched anywhere.

The more commonly used cooperative spectrum from this group evokes specific musical interest and musical psychology. The high to middle range cooperative spectrum involving the *liuqin* (high-range curved-back plucked lute), the *yangqin* (the grand hammered dulcimer), and the *pipa* (the curve-backed grand lute) spans a range of effects to the audience. It can provide a wide range from cold and dry sound to somewhat heated sound, but the real warmth does not begin to be detected until the *zhongruan* (the mid to low range flat-back round lute) joins in. This is ironical. The *sanxian* (the bass long-stringed membrane-resonator lute), the *zheng* (the open-stringed zither with a large and long resonator providing a broad range of tones from low to high), the *se* (the even-larger open-string zither with a long resonator), and the *daruan* (the bass flat-backed round lute) provide a whole range of powerful low frequency for outlining harmonic or melodic skeleton in compositions, and for mood setting. Strong characters in different ranges can be handled forcefully with the *liuqin* and the *sanxian* when their tones become associated with specific characters. Moving and unstable musical motives are more easily handled with the *qin* (the unique instrument offering five octaves of open-string, full-stopped, and harmonics tones), the *zheng*, and the *se*.

The practice of using the tanbo tonal spectrum as fundamental to the orchestra is reasonably popular, but the practice can certainly be improved several fold. A good example is offered by the use of plucked strings as a fundamental tonal spectrum by Liu Wenjin in "The Unforgettable Water-Splashing Festival." Several movements of that piece truly show the power of the spectrally versatile tanbo group. Ma Shenglong and Gu Guanren in "Fishing Song of the East China Sea" used this group successfully in rhythmic functions as a group. But it can be said that it was a more limited use compared with what this group offers acoustically and in terms of evocable musical psychology.

The spectrum of the tanbo group and that of the western symphony (the violin group) are easily combined. This is of interest to composers writing for the symphony category. From the angle of psychology, the plucked string group enhances the power of the violin group with its tonal spectrum (both a result of the wave form and the attacks offered by the performance techniques). If we can just improve on the use of the shengguan group, the complementarity between the shengguan and the tanbo is more than natural.

The tantiao family of *pipa*, *liuqin* and other have acoustical radiation on stage of the dipolar type. This means it makes no difference whether they are placed on the left side or the right side of the stage. On the other hand, if they are placed in the middle facing the audience, the effects are weakest. Problems such as these do not require large amounts of experiments to solve because the theory and common sense already exist.

THE SPECIAL COLORS

Having proposed the fundamental tonal spectrum for the Chinese orchestra we will discuss the role of the other instruments as special color instruments.

The *huqin* vertical fiddles are fabulous instruments as we all know, but acoustically they are not the group to be used as a fundamental spectral group. The popular solo *erhu* has unbelievable penetrating power in the orchestra. They also have their power in a group. But from the angle of orchestral efficiency, the *erhu* group is better accompanied than serving as fundamental tonal spectrum of an orchestra. In a concert hall the ear can tract pitch, tone color and dynamic nuances of instrumental tones with speed and precision. It has been recognized that the ear is most effective with tones consisting of specific harmonic makeup. The ear reacts favorably to the solo *erhu* spectrum but less so to an ensemble *erhu* spectrum. The same is true of the *zhonghu*, the mid-range *erhu*, and the *dahu*, the low-range *huqin*. This phenomenon has to do with the relative strength of the lower partials with respect to the upper, and the pattern in which the upper partials fall off. In terms of orchestral acoustics, the *huqin* (especially the membrane-resonator huqin) does not perform in the fundamental tonal spectrum role compared with the solo (or duet) role. On the other hand, the shengguan and the tanbo groups do an outstanding job as orchestral basis as far as the ear and the brain are concerned. The same is true of the violin group. The reasons are strictly one of musical psychology that is driven by acoustics.

These considerations have widespread implications. The acoustic angle directly affects the analysis of musical psychology before any cultural filtering enters in. These considerations allow orchestras to be designed with a high benefit-to-cost ratio.

Having said that the huqin group did not qualify for a fundamental orchestral spectrum, I must say that the *erhu* group in terms of an *erhu* ensemble (not in an orchestra) has tremendous potential. The format of *erhu* ensemble (in unison or in duet) as in "Wave after Wave of Golden Wheat" (Wang Guotong and Li Xiuqi) has its artistic appeal. The *erhu* group singing the South-of-Yangzi styled passage in "Fishing Song of the East China Sea" (Ma Shenglong and Gu Guanren) can never be forgotten. These are examples of excellent use of the *erhu* group with out subjecting them to the task of orchestral basis. The *erhu* solo in "Longhua Pagoda" (He Zhanhao) in the most depictive passage is also acoustically valid with a Western orchestral basis.

The percussion music of China as a separate musical entity has established itself artistically beyond any doubt. Its status is unmatched by the percussion music of the Western genre. The artistic success of the Chinese percussion music hinges on several crucial features. First, it is a living ensemble. From the South to the North, and from the West to the East, Chinese percussion music is always played in an ensemble. In most instances, the ensemble depends on a few critical instruments. These instruments are so critical to the ensemble that the ensemble is handicapped without any one of them. These whole combinations probably achieve the highest level in conceptual flexibility. This high degree of flexibility and creativity surpasses the achievements of the shengguan group or the tanbo group. This creativity of the percussion group was attained in history and to a large degree preserved in the living music today. We must not in our orchestral composition suppress or limit this creativity, and we should become inspired by this musical and acoustical creativity in our treatment of the shengguan and the tanbo - fundamental tonal spectrum - groups. The *paigu* as a melodic and rhythmic soloist is highly attractive, but a successful orchestral composition should not be dependent solely on a *paigu* solo or the support of limited segments of folk percussion oral patterns. Secondly, Chinese percussion music has its definite philosophy on pitch space. The development of the shengguan music and the tanbo music can be inspired by this pitch space concept, and capitalize on the magnitude of change, the rhythmic breadth, and the emphasis on the use of the sub-spaces. The predictable changes in pitch space of the *xiaoluo* which glides upward and the *daluo* which glides downward are excellent examples of this systematic concept. It is this systematic concept which we can utilize in the union of the shengguan, tanbo, and percussion groups.

In this system we place the *yangqin*, the *bawu*, and the *xiao* in the front center of the stage. The *bawu* and the *xiao* being directly behind the *yangqin* in the first row of the shengguan group which occupies the center quadrant of the stage, with the percussion directly behind the shengguan group in the same quadrant. The shengguan instruments are arranged as follows: *yu* and *sheng* are directly behind the *bawu* and the *xiao*. Here the *yu* performs more melodic functions and the *sheng* performs more harmonic function among the free-reeded mouth organs. The last row of the shengguan group consists of the bass *houguan*, the *guan*, the *di*, the *haidi* and the *suona*.

To the left of the stage are the tanbo with movable pitch and to the right of the stage are the tanbo of primarily the *pipa* family. The front row of the left group are the *qin*, the python-skin *hulei*, the python-skin *qinqin*, the *sanxian* and the *zhonghu*. The second row of the left group are the *zheng*, the *konghou*, and the bass *se*.

To the right of the stage we place the *liuqin*, the *pipa*, the *zhongruan* and the *daruan*.

THE LANGUAGE OF THE MUSIC

The pitch combinations in our compositions are not the source of our musical space. In Chinese culture, the musical space is decided by specific measures. The relationship between points in the space possess special meanings. This includes a cultural meaning, and a compositional meaning. The language here is determined by musical intervals. The musical space can be divided several ways, but the Chinese way of interval language is one that transcends scale. This is why analyzing Chinese music using a scale approach always meets with failure. We encounter the same problem in writing Chinese orchestral music. If our musical thinking becomes one of scale, we lose sensitivity for the energy of change contained in our musical language.

Let us look at a common problem. Are octaves equal? In many compositions, it is obvious that octaves are equal in the musical space of the composer. In reality, this is an oversimplification of our thought. From the larger compositions like "Meihua Sannong" to the nice and short "New Year's Eve," the octaves are unequal. The octaves of *yu-yu, zhi-zhi* in "Meihua Sannong" and the *gong-gong, shang-shang* of "New Year's Eve," a different space is extracted. We see numerous ensemble versions of "Meihua Sannong" which alters completely the broad octave space of the musical language. This occurs in the ensemble arrangement. The musical space is all of a sudden compressed, and the musical interest killed. "New Year's Eve" is a composition for the solo *erhu.* The ensemble arrangements for the Western string orchestra did not further the musical language. Some *yangqin* accompaniments also confused the complementarity of the two instruments and their spatial contrast. Further, the emphasis and balance of harmonic and melodic intervals are often neglected.

Interval dominates our musical language. This is particularly true of Chinese music. In many text books of music, the first concept introduced is that of the scale. This is highly inappropriate in view of the importance of the musical intervals over scale in Chinese music. In fact the new direction of music today is towards broadening the musical space available to us and the logical expansion is one built on intervals. The intervals are much more fundamental building blocks of music than scale. Further, since the intervals dominate our musical language, the temperaments directly control the balance between physical harmony and artistry. In recent centuries, the European musicians emphasized the equal temperament system, but it is a small blip in the music history of mankind. In reality the use of the equal temperament system is a simplification of our musical space. It has become monotonous and artistically limited in the subconscious realm of our brains. Composers for the Chinese orchestra must pay attention to this point - effectively utilize natural intervals and the incredible experience of a very broad tonal spectral system. The technique of resonant counterpoint under concert hall reverberation with equal-tempered intervals and natural intervals is also effective. The natural intervals of Wang Guotong and the equal-tempered intervals of Zhou Guangren in the resonance of "Fantasy on the Sanmen Gorge" (Liu Wenjin) produced precisely this effect.

We have analyzed the roles of the shengguan and the tanbo groups as fundamental tonal spectrum instruments for the Chinese orchestra. They have used in those roles in an incredible number of Chinese orchestras from historical times to the present. And yet in the confusion of modern times we tend to ignore their natural roles. From the standpoint of concert-hall acoustics, they once again stand out, in a room-averaged[2] fashion, as the most usable fundamental tonal spectrum instruments for the

---

[2] Room-averaged results approximate the true effects we hear in a concert hall or in a room, and are thus the important numbers.

Chinese orchestra. The best acoustical combination utilizing the two groups has the shengguan group enclosed in a middle fan space. To the left of the stage are the *qin*, the *zheng*, the *hulei*, the *qinqin*, the *sanxian*, the *konghou*, the *zhonghu* and the *se*. In the front stage center is the *yangqin*. To the right of the stage are the *liuqin*, the *pipa*, the *zhongruan* and the *daruan*. Here the *yangqin*, the *liuqin*, the *pipa*, the *zhongruan* and the *daruan* belong to high, middle, and low range of plate vibration resonators. The *zheng*, the *qin*, the *se*, and the *konghou* belong to long-stringed middle-and low-ranged plate resonators with movable-pitch performing techniques. (Their special position is due to these characteristic performance methods which allow the performance of highly unstable musical motives). The python-skin *hulei*, the python-skin *qinqin*, the *sanxian* and the *zhonghu* all belong to low- and middle-ranged membrane resonators.

Characteristic instruments for solo or small group use including the *zhuihu*, the *jinghu*, the *erhu*, the *banhu*, or even the *gaohu* (the acoustical data on the *gaohu* indicates that this is a member of the *huqin* family that is usable in a fundamental tonal spectral group) are not intended for use as fundamental spectral instruments for the orchestra. When they are used they could be put in the proximity of the broad-spectral *yangqin*, and the *bawu* or the *xiao*. The *bawu* and the *xiao*, if used, are directly behind the *yangqin*. The *yu* and the *sheng* in modern days are usually all called *sheng* regardless of the number of reeded pipes. Our distinction here for the purpose of orchestration is to put the harmonic usage on the side of the *haidi*, the *suona*, the *liuqin* and the *pipa*, and to put the melodic functions (those of the *yu*) on the side of the *di*, the *guan*, the *zheng* and the *konghou*.

Regarding the tuning of the string instruments, it is very important to respect the natural intervals and the non-equal-tempered performance. The *zhongruan* should be tuned using an alternating fifth-fourth tuning, and not fifth-fifth. Here the *zhongruan* is an energetic instrument as we discussed when we analyzed the acoustical and music-psychological role, therefore, we should not treat it strictly as a component of our harmony. This will release the instrument into its more natural role. The compass is not as important as the precision in the natural intervals.

Based in acoustics and based in musical psychology we build the tonal spectra of the Chinese orchestra using the shengguan and the tanbo bases. The music language follows the same threads of thought, to beautify our musical space, to break out of the limits of scale and equal-temperament, and to unlock the new era of orchestral music which inherits the past and inspires the future.

REFERENCES

Fang, Pu-dong, private communication (1978).

Huadong Xiqu Yanjiuyuan (Institute for Theatrical Music of Eastern China), *Huadong Xiqu Juzhong Jieshao* (Introduction to the Types of Theatrical Styles of Eastern China), Xin Wenyi Chubanshe (New Literature and Arts Publisher), Shanghai (1955).

Jiangsu Nanbu Minjian Xiqu Shuochang Yinyue Ji (A Collection of Theatrical and Ballad Singing Music of Southern Jiangsu), edited by the Committee on Music Research of the Jiangsu Province, Yinyue Chubanshe (Music Publisher), Beijing (1955).

Lai, Chun-yue, "Lao Liuban," *Chinese Music*, Vol. 2, No. 4, p. 47 (1979).

Lee, Yuan-yuan, "The Liuyeqin and Wang Huiran," *Chinese Music*, Vol. 2, No. 2, p. 6 (1979).

Liu, Wenjin, private communication (1978).

Liu, Wenjin, private communication (1979).

Qi, Rushan, *Guoju Yishu Huikao* (1949).

Shen, Sin-yan, Foundations of the Chinese Orchestra I, *Chinese Music*, **2**, 32 (1979).

Shen, Sin-yan, Foundations of the Chinese Orchestra II, *Chinese Music*, **3**, 16 (1980).

Shen, Sin-yan, What Makes Chinese Music Chinese?, *Chinese Music*, **4**, 23 (1981).

Shen, Sin-yan, Instruments of the Chinese Orchestra, *Chinese Music*, **7**, 33 (1984).

Shen, Sin-yan, The Music of the Chinese Music Society of North America, *Chinese Music*, **9**, 3 (1986).

The Science of Fangsheng Performance

The *fangsheng*, or the square mouthorgan, is a very special and important instrument for composers. In order to write effectively for this instrument, I studied its performance a few decades ago. In so doing I fell in love with this classical instrument. I will discuss here the logic of the square mouthorgan, the *fangsheng*, in its design science, its fingering, and relevant harmonic information. The performance of the *gong*, *shang*, *jue*, *zhi*, and *yu* harmonies will be carefully analyzed. The "do's and don'ts" for using the *fangsheng* by composers of orchestral music are discussed.

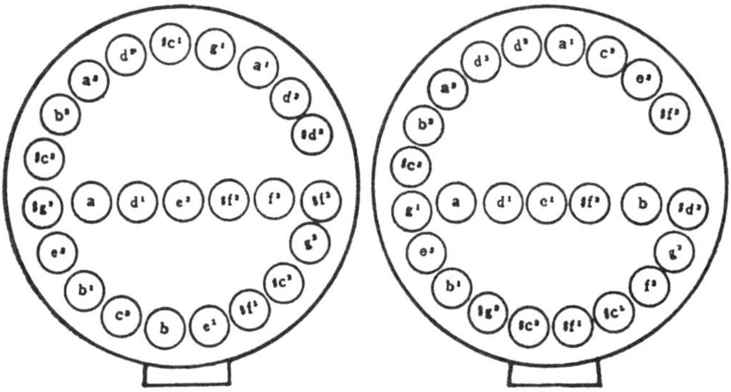

There are two basic designs of the *sheng* used in the Chinese orchestra: the *yuansheng* (round) and the *fangsheng* (square). The *yuansheng* is somewhat more common throughout the many Provinces and has an "inverted reversed e" circular arrangement. Shown are the pitch arrangements of a number of common *yuansheng*. The *fangsheng* is popular in Northern China and has now become popular among orchestral players in many major orchestras and is manufactured by most large instrument factories all across China. The *fangsheng* has its pitches arranged in three parallel rows. The pipes in the first row, the row closest in the mouthpiece, are controlled by the thumbs. The second row is controlled by the index fingers, and the third row is principally controlled by the middle finger, assisted by the fourth and the fifth fingers. The reeded pipes are arranged such that the bass pipes are in the middle of each row and the pitches go progressively higher as one moves away from the center. The pitches of adjacent rows are a major second apart, like on the yangqin (the grand dulcimer) where adjacent notes on a single bridge are separated by a full step. What we will discuss below is the popular 36-reed *fangsheng* which uses a closed-tube structure in which the free reed in each reed-pipe coupling becomes in resonance with the air column when the air-hole is opened by a key. For purposes of the ease of discussion, we will adopt the following fingering diagram, where the first row controlled by the two thumbs is at the bottom of the diagram and the lowest notes with the largest keys are shown with more space on the diagram for us to recognize the center right away. The second row controlled by the index fingers is placed right above the first, and the third follows after a slight separation space to represent the physical space on the *fangsheng*. The left half of the *fangsheng* is usually controlled by the left hand and the right half by the right hand.

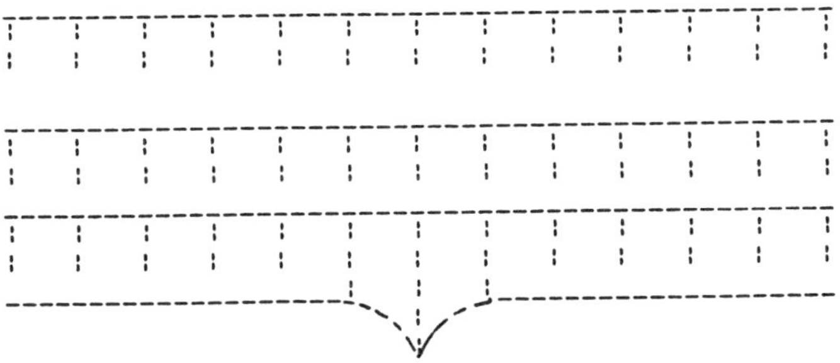

To proceed with the discussion, we might reacquaint ourselves with the commonly used harmonies which form the basis of all Chinese music (see Shen, 1981). The five harmonies in any one field of gong consist of

zhi:

(tonic on fifth of *gong*)-(fourth above tonic)-(fifth above tonic)-(octave)

shang:

(tonic on second of *gong*)-(fourth above tonic)-(fifth above tonic)-(octave)

yu:

(tonic on sixth of *gong*)-(fourth above tonic)-(fifth above tonic)-(octave)

jue:

(tonic on third of *gong*)–(fourth above tonic)–(minor sixth above tonic)–(octave)

and *gong*:

(tonic on *gong*)–(major third above tonic)–(fifth above tonic)–(octave).

The *zhi*, *shang*, and *yu* harmonies emphasize the fourth and the fifth for decorating the octave, thus forming a major second defined by subtracting a fourth from a fifth. The *jue* harmony emphasizes the minor sixth and the fourth in decorating the octave, thus producing a minor third, the first harmonic interval in Chinese music (see Huang, 1978), and the *gong* harmony uses a fifth and a major third to decorate the octave, forming another minor third between the fifth and the major third. These harmonies form the basis of melodic progression and modulation. They provide a broad and highly creative harmonic space yet fully equipped with plausible logical framework. The classical western harmonies based on the major and minor triads are a subset of the Chinese harmonies (see Shen, 1983). All of the inversions of the basic harmonies and their associated complex chords must be handled by the *fangsheng* in orchestral music and solo works, and this must be accomplished for all keys.

It is important to understand the symmetry of the *fangsheng* with respect to its center. Let us for purposes of clarity call the left-hand columns L1 through L6 in the order away from the center, and call the right-hand columns R1 through R6 also in the order away from the center. The pitches of corresponding left and right columns differ by a semitone as follows:

(1) R1 and R2 are higher than L1 and L2 by a semitone,
(2) R3 and R4 are lower than L3 and L4 by a semitone, and
(3) R5 and R6 are higher than L5 and L6 by a semitone.

There is another important symmetry which comes in handy at performance time. The rectangular block of L3L4L5L6 is the mirror image of the block R1R2R3R4 except it is one octave higher. The block L1L2L3L4 is the mirror image of R3R4R5R6 except it is one octave lower. The diagram below illustrates the first mirror image using the gong of D as an example. Here the pitch designation is relative. Upper case is used to represent pitches an octave lower than the lower case.

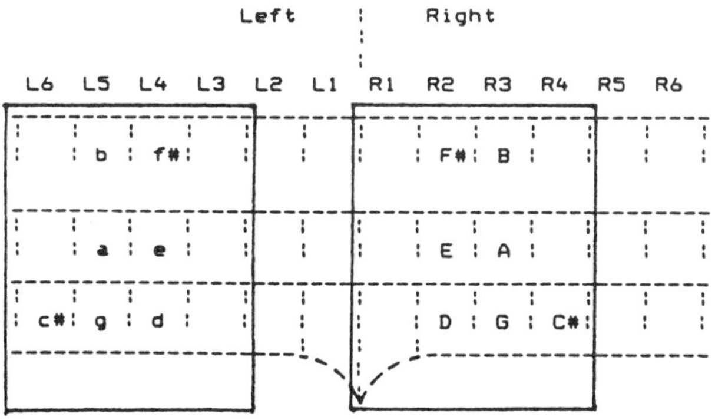

gong of D

With the above symmetries in mind, all we need to focus on is any <u>one half</u> of the *fangsheng* at a time[1]. The diagram below illustrates the relationship between columns. Since all adjacent pitches within each column are a full step apart, all we need to worry about are the interval between the end of a column and the beginning of another column. This interval remains a major second with two-column blocks, e.g. between L1 and L2, between L3 and L4, and so on. If one moves back and forth between the left and the right or the right and the left two column-blocks at a time, this interval is also a major second, i.e. (1) the end of L2 and the beginning of R3 are separated by a major second, and (2) the end of R4 and the beginning of L5 are separated by a major second.

Now that we have defined the complete internal structure of the fingering, it suffices to note that the lowest pitch on the common 36-reed *fangsheng* is the G below middle C.

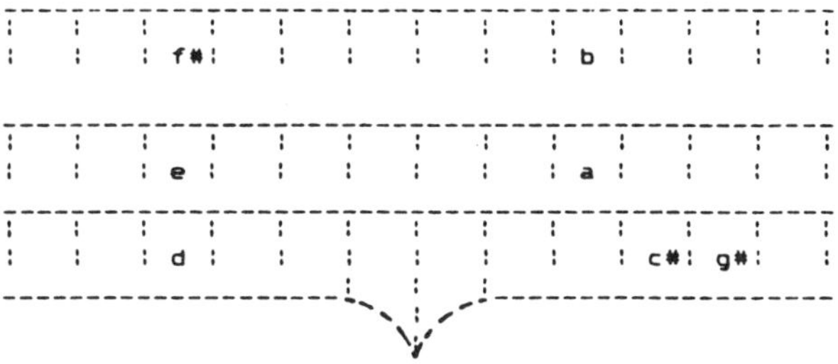

gong of A

[1] The *fangsheng's* ability to allow us to think about half of the instrument at a time comes from its clever use of symmetry.

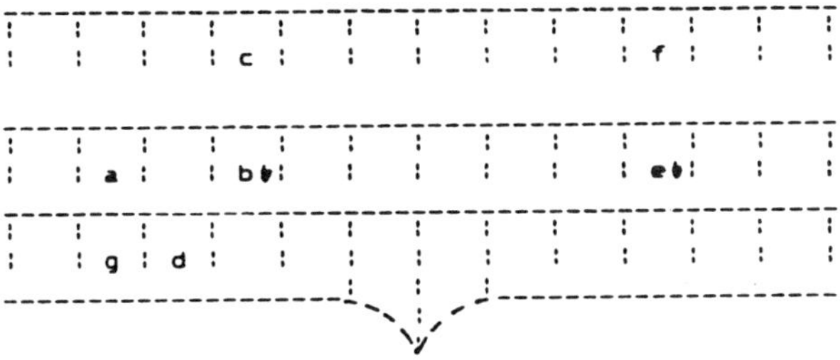

gong of B^b

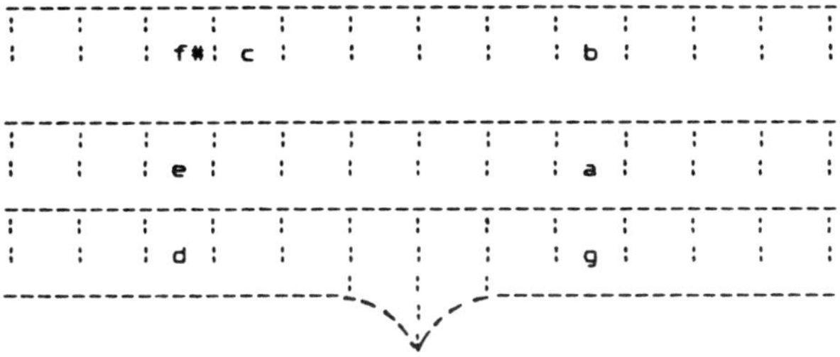

gong of G

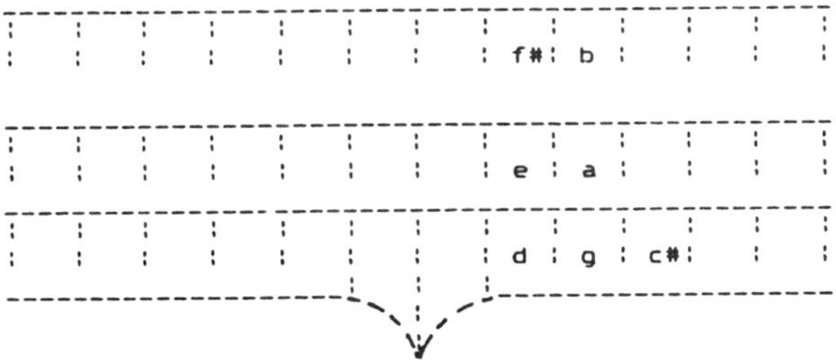

gong of D

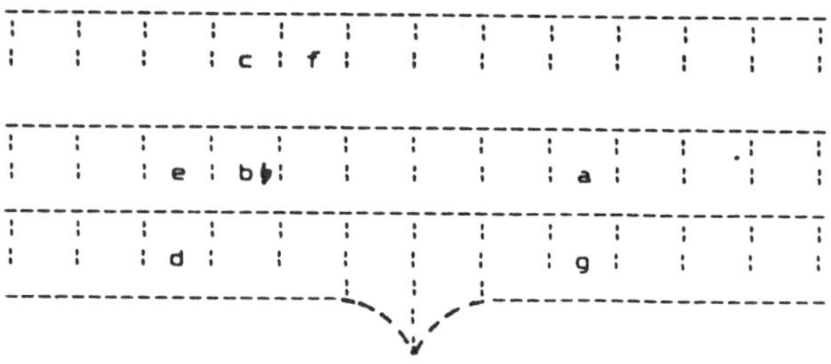

gong of F

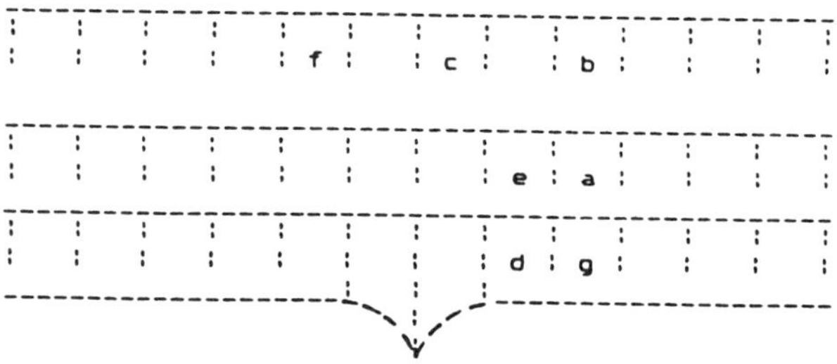

gong of C

As we have shown, like many Chinese musical instruments, the *fangsheng* is an interval instrument[2], i.e. its performance technique is based on intervals as opposed to the piano where the white keys define the C major scale and the black keys provide the altered steps. This is really not surprising since the basis of Chinese melodic progression is a set of intervals, and successful orchestration and composition depend on a creative compromise between the harmonic and the discord in the

[2] As opposed to a scale instrument.

creation of an impressive perception of tonal sequences which manifest as intervals.

Given the interval rules, we can now map out the fingering for the common harmonies. In the field of gong of D we have A *zhi*.

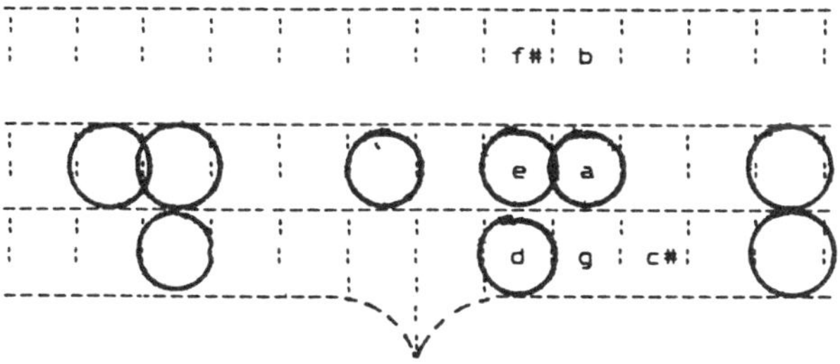

gong of D

E *shang*.

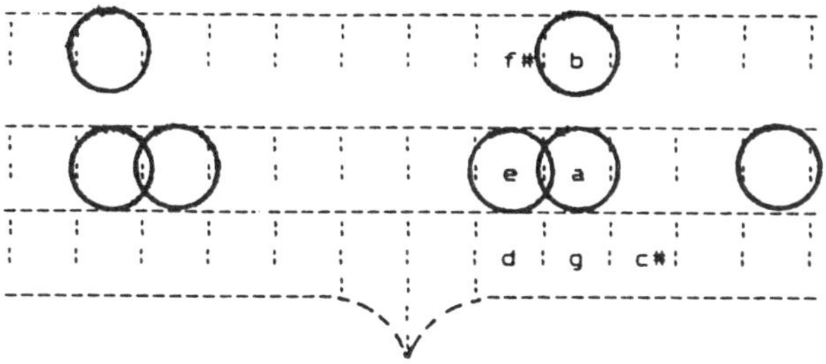

gong of D

B *yu*.

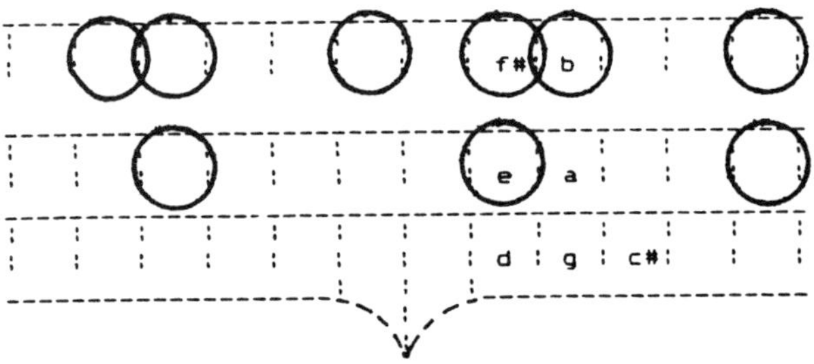

gong of D

F# *jue*.

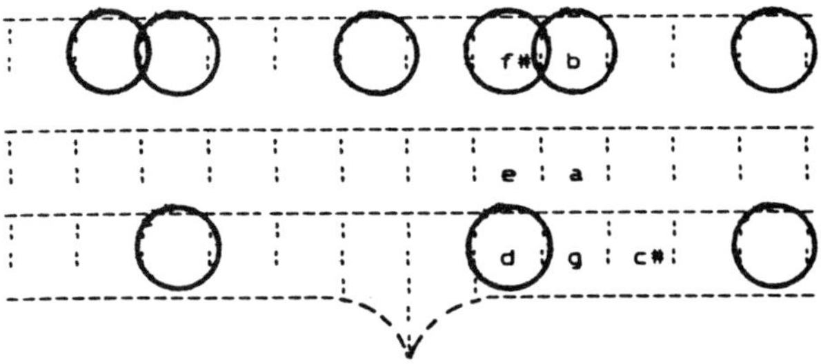

gong of D

and D *gong*.

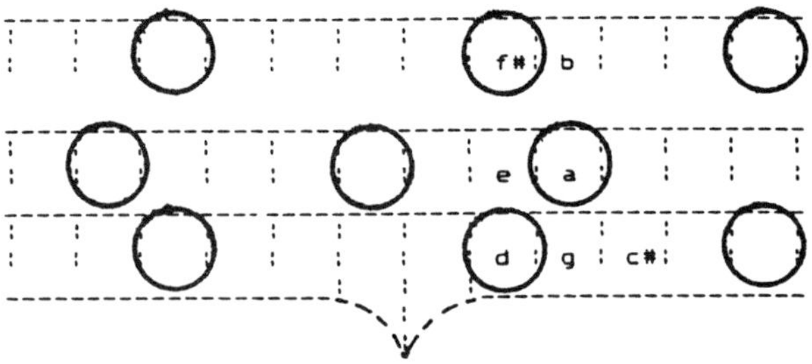

gong of D

In the field of *gong* of B-flat we have F *zhi.*

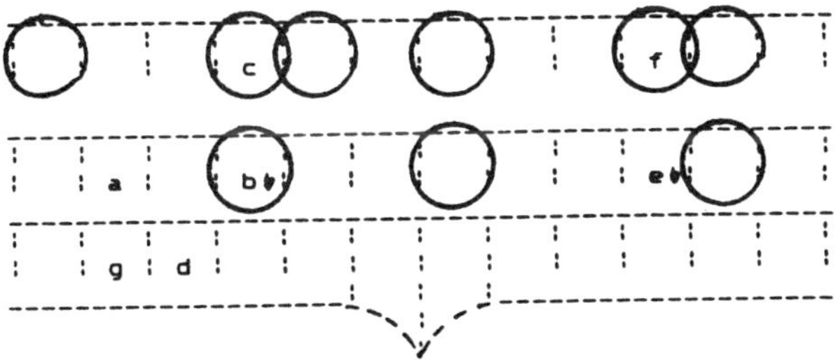

gong of B^b

C *shang.*

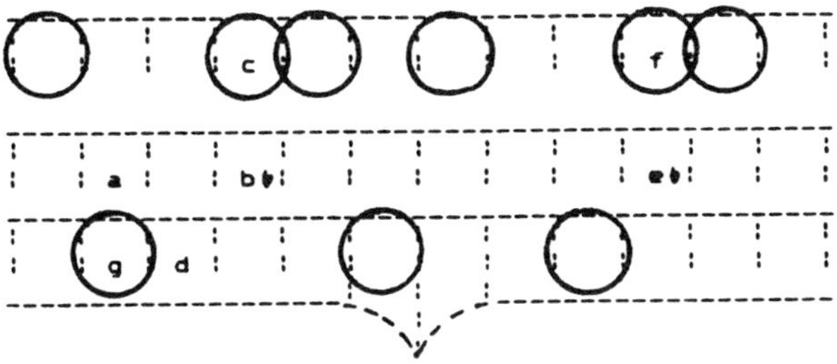

gong of B^b

G *yu.*

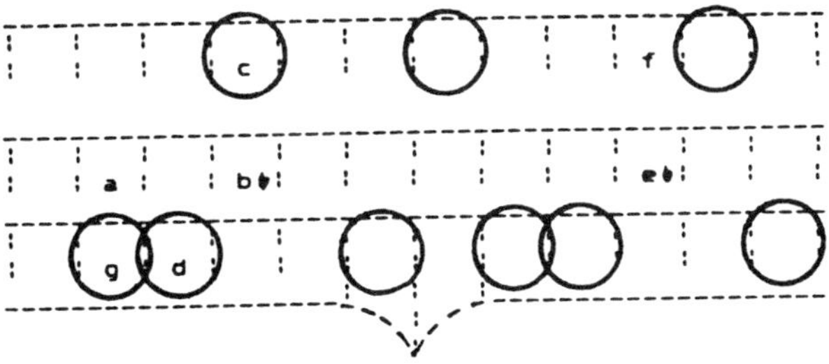

gong of B^b

D *jue*.

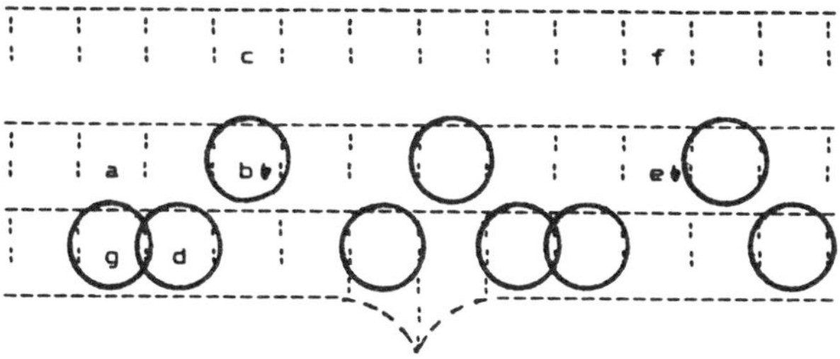

gong of B^b

and B-flat *gong*.

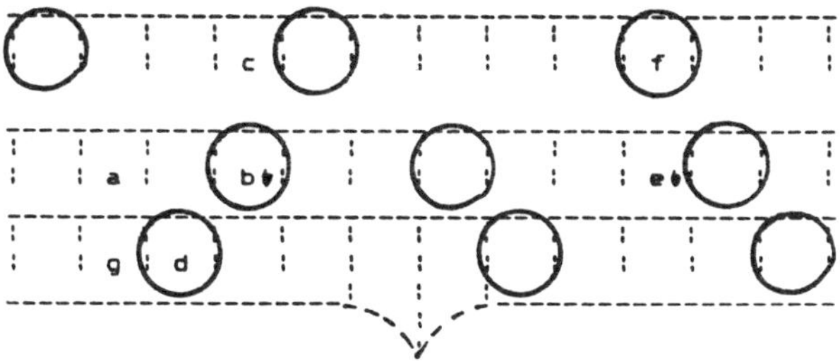

gong of B^b

Except for the performance of Western music, the *fangsheng* really should not be used too frequently in compositions for performing strictly equal-tempered chromatic passages. Since the *fangsheng* is not a flexible-pitched instrument like the *qin*, the *erhu*, the *pipa*, or the *suona*, its music further emphasizes harmony. In fact the *sheng* family was the first wind instrument that allowed any number of tones to be sounded at the same time. The flexible-pitched instruments emphasize tonal manipulation in Chinese music and the sheng family emphasizes intervals and harmony. When the *sheng* is used in the orchestra it is very important to make sure that the temperament system of the music is followed in the strictest manner. In Cantonese music when the *gaohu* or the *houguan* play two different required pitches between the gong's major third and perfect fifth, never allow the *sheng* to destroy the natural harmony by playing the fourth above the gong all by itself. It simply makes everything out of tune. A recent release by the Hong Kong Record Company on Cantonese music had "The Peacock Spreads Its Tail" on it, which made the above error in orchestration.

The *fangsheng* is a powerful instrument when used harmonically to enhance the dynamics of passages. In the last part of "The Flowers are Blooming and the Moon is Full" where the *sheng* successively increases its volume in performing simple supportive harmony, the results are spectacular.

REFERENCES

Shen Sin-yan, "What Makes Chinese Music Chinese", *Chinese Music*, 4, 23 (1981).

Huang Xiang-peng, "Study of the Development of the Chinese Scale System Using Known Acoustical Materials of the Neolithic and the Bronze Ages", *Yinyue Luncong*, 1, 184 (1978) and 3, 126 (1980).

Shen Sin-yan, "The Moon on High - Techniques of Chinese Classical Composition", *Chinese Music*, **6**, 3 and **6**, 23 (1983).

■

The Artistic Pathway of Chinese Music - On Analyzing the Works of Hua Yanjun (A Bing)

On the eve of the 100th Anniversary[1] of A Bing's birth I came to Wuxi, Jiangsu, China. In A Bing's home town, I had a chance to draw on several decades of Chinese music and cultural acoustics research, in elucidating the pathway through which the artistic thoughts behind Chinese music have taken. Compositions in the A Bing System radiate his specially "A Bing" acoustical space, and utilize completely his powerful fixed position glissando performance on silk strings. I will explain in detail and in layman's terms how the aesthetic philosophy of Chinese music can be properly appreciated today, and will establish the principal theoretical features of A Bing's composition system.

THE ROLE OF RESEARCH

Why the need to research, in particular, the works of Hua Yanjun (A Bing)? Our discussion encompasses various

---

[1] Keynote Lecture at the 100th Anniversary International Conference of the Birth of Hua Yanjun (A Bing), Wuxi, Jiangsu, China. (Lecture translated from the Chinese by Wu Zhiqi).

perspectives; the development of music, composition, performance as well as artistic quality. It was in the 1950s when I first became acquainted with the compositions of Hua Yanjun, as well as documents pertaining to him, that I began to truly appreciate the value of musicology. The increased appreciation of Chinese music today and the works of Hua Yanjun owes much to the research of musicologists such as Yang Yinliu, Cao Anhe, Chu Shizhu, and Li Songshou, without whom we would never have been able to commemorate the birth centenary of the composer. In particular, Li Songshou was the one to have brought his great friend and teacher to the attention of the world. Meticulous musicological research not only complements society's awareness of artistic quality, but also lends impetus to the development of music as an art form.

For the past decade, the impact of the so-called 'popular' and 'serious' music on society has provoked much controversy (See Shen, Zhongguo Yinyuejie Dui Renlei Ying Fu De Zeren, 1982; Shen, 1985; Shen, 1996; Shen, 1999). In reality, both serious and popular music have a complementary rather than conflicting function in society. We have to recognize their differing value as well as function. Other than entertainment, it is the cogitative aspect of classical music, which fosters self-betterment that sets it apart from popular music. The works of Hua Yanjun have precisely such an effect.

Besides conveying infectious and pleasurable feelings, the acoustical logic of classical music is capable of regulating the development of the brain. Listening to music like *The Moon Mirrored in Erquan*, *Listen to the Pine*, and *Fantasy on the*

Sanmen Gorge, enhances the development of a more objective and perspective vision. Good music helps us remove all obstacles by providing a clearing path for rigorous intellectual preparation. In solving problems pertaining to either the natural or social sciences, listening to beautiful music of a highly enlightening and mercurial nature is the best way of equipping myself with a clear mindset for effective analytical discourse. American scientists recently conducted a series of education experiments, in which the problem solving skills of a group of students were gauged before and after listening to a work by Mozart. Apparently, it was discovered that the problem solving skills of the students improved after listening to the music of Mozart. Perhaps this is due to the dialectic nature of classical music, which facilitates methodical cogitation, thus increasing the reasoning capacity of the brain. Conversely, the repetitive structure of western European and American popular music does not convey the same effect as Mozart. The classical music of China, such as *Fishermen Song of the East China Sea* (See Shen, in *The Shanghai Traditional Orchestra and He Wu-qi*, 1982), *Fantasy on the Sanmen Gorge*, *Echo of the Flute and Drum at Sunset*, *The Moon on High*, *The Moon Mirrored in Erquan*, *Listen to the Pine* (See University of California, 1990), etc., expresses the structural beauty and cogitative nature of Chinese music. Such music not only induces concentration, but also heightens the understanding of Mankind's place within the cosmos by bringing himself into a higher spiritual realm. The origin of this type of psychological effect needs to be discussed from a perspective of the relationship between basic acoustics and culture.

The study of acoustics is a part of physical science, yet it is cultural acoustics that serves the needs of musicology and music appreciation. From the perspective of physics, the intervals of an octave and fifth are considered harmonious, but taking a cultural acoustical viewpoint, the interval of a third or even second can be similarly regarded as so. Harmonic preferences are determined by cultural practices, the disparity between the musical traditions of each cultural system being determined by cultural acoustics.

The range of harmonic intervals, mode of notation, and spectrum for orchestration favored by a cultural system is quantifiable by the science of cultural acoustics. These considerations lay the foundation of all music theory and the relationship between different cultural systems. The various aspects of orchestral fundamental spectra and music notational systems of the Chinese orchestra had been previously discussed elsewhere (refer to the second issue of the 1989 edition of People's Music, pages 2-4, *On the Acoustical Space of The Chinese Orchestra*). Here I will use the works of Hua Yanjun to illustrate the cultural acoustical science of music composition and the solutions to various inherent conceptual problems.

I would first like to emphasize the distinction between the concepts of "qudiao" in classical Chinese music and melodic structure in western music. In Chinese music, there are various culturally implicated nuances that need not be written, as they vary with each performance. A similar analogy will be the lack of tempo indication, for one should not let the physical form of the written notes hamper creative potential. Now this is a very important concept that is necessary for comprehending the philosophy of Chinese music and its vitality as an art form. For the lack of tempo indication is in fact a manifestation of the conceptual basis of music being without eternal form, having instead ever-regenerating life cycles. Written notation serves only as a annotation device for an era, each era favoring different methods of annotation, and should hence only function as a tool for fostering creativity, rather than forge boundaries that restrict creativity. Similarly, each era and locality have distinct preferences with regards to the establishment of melodic structure and melodic decoration. If one were to write down every nuance, then the music of China will lose its artistic vitality.

Presently, western classical music is primarily performed using written notation, with every performance direction indicated, because conceptually, these are part of melodic structure. Anyone brought up with the performance traditions of western classical music will be astounded by the structural complexity of the work "Lao Liuban" (The Old Six Measures) performed by a Chinese musician reading the seemingly sparse *gongchi* notation that is totally devoid of tempo indication and performance direction. Hence we need to reiterate the concept that the acoustical space of Chinese music contains culturally implicated nuances, which can be inferred through the study of cultural acoustics and a broadened concept of harmony and harmonic sense (See for example Shen, 1979; Shen, 1980; Shen, 1981; Shen, 1987). Such is cultural acoustics. The beauty and profoundness of Chinese music lies within its inherent capacity for cogitation and the artistry of its acoustics. If we were to individually isolate the works of Hua Yanjun as an artistic system, we will find that it possesses a close affinity with the science of cultural acoustics. Most of all, it is the unique tonal spectrums and artistic cogitative expressiveness in his performances that warrant our study of his music.

THE 'A BING SYSTEM' -PRACTICAL IMPLICATIONS ON CHINESE MUSICAL COGITATION, COMPOSITION AND PERFORMANCE

All of A Bing's compositions share intimate relationships in cultural acoustics. The acoustical space of A Bing's works originates from the culture of south of the Yangzi, the region known as Jiangnan, but differs from the conventional folk music of the region. The *zhi* harmony is of principal importance in Chinese music, especially in the indigenous music of Jiangnan. For it is the acoustical foundation of the *zhi* harmony in the 'Hua Yanjun System' that expands and artistically utilizes the colors of acoustical space, thus forming the acoustical space of the Hua Yanjun System through the "*zhi* progressing to *gong*" harmonic cycle. Indeed, his artistic methodology and creativity embodies the very essence of musical cogitation within the Chinese cultural system.

The beauty of Hua Yanjun's works lies in their inherent cogitative quality. Gradual unfolding of emotional expression is accompanied by each phrase appropriately playing its part in the overall structural cogitation of the work. Chinese and foreign musicologists devoted to the structural analysis of the best known work of Hua Yanjun, *The Moon Mirrored in Erquan*, often examine it from a perspective of a variation on a theme. In their studies, an erroneous conceptual approach is often taken as a result of the lack of proper understanding of Chinese musical culture. From the standpoint of western melodic structural sense, the themes within his music are ambiguous, yet the key acoustical space and harmony are clear. This is a common phenomenon found in the great classics of ancient Chinese music.

Chinese classics such as *The Moon Mirrored in Erquan*, the ancient classic *The Moon on High*, and *Echo of the Flute and Drum at Sunset* (also known as *Music at Sunset*), etc., all possess a gradual unfolding thematic exposition, but have a broader harmonic structure as compared to most western classical music. In *The Moon on High*, we have:

Other than the "mi" and "la" that I have circled which are skeletons of the melodic progression and cannot be altered, all other notes can take multiple combinations, and will be different with each performance, with each space-time and with each group of players. Therefore what we have notated above should never be treated as a "melody". Forcibly noting down every musical nuance will only serve to destroy artistic intent and expression, resulting in a retrogression of musical expedience. The adaptability of the Chinese harmonic system is in some ways akin to jazz, but is very different in terms of ideology and manner of execution.

The structure of European classical music rests upon the foundation of the cultural background developed in recent history, which evolved from medieval monody to the harmonic based polyphony structure of today. Hence, much emphasis is placed on melodic, thematic and key juxtaposition. Melodic structure aside, importance is also attached to a quantized contrast of accentuation and tempo. When applying such disposition to Chinese music, a thematic structure needs to be unnaturally forged, along with a consequent quantization of melodic structure, of tempo and of accentuation. In performances of the last 5 decades, the original natural seven-part exposition of *The Moon Mirrored in Erquan* (For formal design, see Ng, 1979) has been simplified into a three-part variation in order to satisfy psychological requirements of quantized aesthetics, which invariably diminishes artistry and cogitative coherence.

The Chinese musical system accepted a very broad harmonic content early in the history of its development, the indigenous music of the various regions conforming to the five cyclic harmonies of the Chinese musical system. This includes all regional music and music of all minorities. The various respective harmonic structures are *zhi, shang, yu, jue* and *gong*. Whenever key notes of any of these harmonic structures are sounded, the effect of cultural acoustics has an allusive influence on other key notes. This practice of harmoniousness and harmonic implications is still present in the cultural acoustics of Russian music (My dear friend Du Yaxiong conducted research on the harmonic preferences of the Russian musical system. It was found, for example, that any component of a major third can be substituted freely by the other components in practice as a result of their inherent allusive quality), but modern western classical musicians have lost it.

As a result of the cyclic pattern of the Chinese harmonic system, key modulation has a dual scientific and aesthetic function, its pattern of expansion and contraction of acoustical and harmonic space being in accordance with an artistic train of thought. It is for this reason that the ancient classic *The Moon on High*, is considered as one of the greatest among the repertoire, as it utilizes the full range of the cyclic harmonic pattern.

For many years, a thorough research on the compositions of Hua Yanjun has yet to be conducted, which can be historically justified. Both international as well as Chinese musicologists are well aware of the fact that as many as more than 200 of Hua Yanjun's works remain unrecorded (*The Moon Mirrored in Erquan, Listen to the Pine, Huge Wave Refines the Sand*, etc., were recorded in 1950). Many thought it a pity that we do not have access to a complete anthology of his works. In fact we have a lot of A Bing, and have yet to even conduct a critical research and examination of the six recorded compositions, giving rise to misconceptions such as dividing *The Moon Mirrored in Erquan* into three variations by forging 'melodic structural contrast'.

The A Bing System radiates the specially "A Bing" acoustical space, and the resonance of his fixed position glissando.

To understand A Bing, you have to understand his acoustical space. The Hua Yanjun System adopts a multipleprong approach in offering the acoustics of the *zhi* harmony[2], but a clear musical objective is always completely evident:

Erquan

Cold Spring Wind

Erquan

Cold Spring Wind

Here, we are unable to discern an unstable quality in the dominant, as is often the case in western music. In many performances of *The Moon Mirrored in Erquan*, a sense of dreariness often pervades, and an apparently slow tempo adopted. Evidently, this shows a lack of appreciation for his music, for the image of a poor, wretched folk musician figures all too strongly, neglecting his embodiment of the spirit of Chinese culture.

According to the Chinese concept of acoustical space, much of the melodic nuances are allusive, although their relationship to each other is clear. All these are evident in the performances and compositions of the Hua Yanjun System. In A Bing's composition, the emotional development is gradual, but when the principal phrase is played:

---

[2] The favorite son of the *zhi-shang-yu-jue-gong* harmony system.

bright separate bowing displays the complete skeleton of the *zhi* harmony. Here he executes with complete assertiveness and bustling emotion. And when he played:

the acoustical thoughts radiate in all solid angles, defining the space of the composition, and defying any purely "melodic" thoughts.

In the cultural acoustical space of ancient music and the Hua Yanjun System, notes which are either specified or alluded show clear indication of the effective artistic combination of creativity and performance. Conversely, the allusive acoustical elements inherent in Chinese acoustical space possess varying pitches which might not necessary be acoustically supplementary. An example will be the do-sol position favored by Hua Yanjun (what would be known to him as the third position), which is of prime importance in the Hua Yanjun System. When composing, he fully utilizes the technique of fixed glissando (See Shen, *On the System of Chinese Fiddles*, 1990) in the position mentioned above, creating an effect of romantic expressiveness. For example, in *Cold Spring Wind* (Hán Chun Feng Qu),

and

are really the same entity. For such composition techniques are unique to both the Hua Yanjun System as well as Chinese music.

The significance of the *zhi* harmony in Chinese music can be compared favorably with the 'major tonality' of western classical music. Its usage among the various regional music of China is statistically far more prevalent than that of the *gong* harmony, and is artistically a key component of music from the Jiangnan region south of the Yangzi, but even more so in the Hua Yanjun System. In *The Moon on High* (Yuè Ér Gao), our complete analysis (See *Chinese Music*, Vol. 6, p. 3-7 and p. 23-31) reveals the musical motive force of the complete composition:

which consists of only three notes. Similarly, we find *Erquan* has a motive skeleton of the "sol" space. The complete composition surrounds the acoustics of the harmony:

and the musical result scores the typical "A Bing". The skeleton combination of *zhi* harmony is :

and the inversions are:

The structure of *Erquan* is built on a "Zhi progression to Gong" on the basis of the zhi harmonic space: on the A Bing erhu the third position "sol" and "do" are both performed with the index finger. In this position the skeleton do-sol-do octave is shared by zhi harmony and the gong harmony.

Within the cultural acoustical space of *Erquan,* the principal musical skeleton is (principal members circled):

+ octave

In the past most analyses focused narrowly on

and the stable form

In reality there were either the introductory phrase or the arrival phrase of A Bing, and are not important in the overall scheme of composition. Its most heavy-weight "sol" paragraphs are summarized here:

We will discuss elsewhere the composition thoughts and structure of this "sol" composition framework.

Where treatment of temperament is concerned, the Hua Yanjun System has many conceptual problems that should be noted. In many performances of the Hua Yanjun repertoire (such as *The Moon Mirrored in Erquan* and *Listen to the Pine*), equal temperament and interval quantization is often employed. The achievement of Hua Yanjun lies in his masterful grasp of performance technique and his treatment of the contradictory coexistence between artistic intervals and other intervals preferred by the Chinese cultural system, and above all, his mastery of music as an art form. His artistic vision penetrates all his other compositions, a perfect continuum of "vision-creativity-execution", indeed, a celebration of musical invention. His strive for precision in the execution of fixed glissando for the minor third mi-sol can be in principle similarly accurately applied to another minor third la-do on the lower string. Yet, his treatment of the other components within the minor third intervals (3 to 5 shown) mentioned above possesses a perpetual continuum, as the movement of the index finger from mi to sol encompasses several infinite intervals. For it is the congruity of art that distinguishes it from physics (Refer to diagram).

3 ------*pivoting note*------ 5

↑ ↑ ↑ ↑ ↑ ↑ ↑ ↑ ↑ ↑ ↑ ↑ ↑

← continuum space →

If the infinite choice of intervals within the continuum space are to be ignorantly bounded by #4, ↑4 or 4, it only shows no understanding of the cultural acoustics of China and an inability to grasp the realm of Chinese musical expression (It happens to many).

The compositions of Hua Yanjun as well as his own performances (the same written music deviates in the hands of different individuals) attain a realm second to no other form of musical expression. For the treatments of "sol", A Bing's free-flowing

(*Erquan*)

and completely unconstrained

(*Listen to the Pine*)

are miles above the following from "Jiangnan Sizhu" (Shanghai Silk & Bamboo)

(*Song of Joy*)

21ST CENTURY AND THE FUTURE OF CHINESE MUSIC - OUR CRITICAL OVERVIEW

In summary of the above discussion, we have brought to light the embodying significance of the Hua Yanjun System in

Chinese culture. The artistic achievement of Hua Yanjun has its basis in the highly integrated ideologue, composition and performing techniques of Chinese music. The influences of western musical traditions have eroded our understanding of our very own musical systems and methodology. The future development of Chinese music will depend on our own holistic view of Chinese culture and mastery of its musical tradition.

An understanding of the Hua Yanjun System provides the commencement for a critical perspective. Our mass exportation of musical talent and compositions has shown their results at international competitions, but only among the western-oriented coterie. The aesthetic criterion employed is not only western-oriented but also far removed from the vista of human civilization. The refutation of superficial, backward cultural ideologue and even unscientific theory is of utmost importance. What should be retained, however, is the holistic philosophy of our artistic Chinese culture - the understanding of the cosmos, an awareness of the place of Mankind in the scheme of things and cultural acoustical theory. Let the gems of our exalted human civilization be internationalized and spread the love of civilization - for all lovers of music should share this crystallization of human civilization. May Chinese musical perspective and performance thrive in the 21st century! By following such an artistic path, Hua Yanjun would have rest in peace and not lived in vain.

REFERENCES

Ng Kok Koon, The Moon Mirrored in Erquan, *Chinese Music*, **2**, 43 (1979).

Shen, Sin-yan, Foundations of the Chinese Orchestra, *Chinese Music*, **2**, 32 (1979).

Shen, Sin-yan, Foundations of the Chinese Orchestra II, *Chinese Music*, **3**, 16 (1980).

Shen, Sin-yan, What Makes Chinese Music Chinese? *Chinese Music*, **4**, 23 (1981).

Shen, Sin-yan, Zhongguo Yinyuejie Dui Renlei Ying Fu De Zeren (in Chinese), *Zhongguo Yinyue*, 1982, No. 2, 18 (1982).

Shen, Sin-yan, The Shanghai Traditional Orchestra and He Wu-qi, *Chinese Music*, **5**, 43 (1982).

Shen, Sin-yan, The Moon on High: Techniques of Chinese Classical Composition, *Chinese Music*, **6**, 3-7 and 23-31 (1983).

Shen, Sin-yan, Instruments of the Chinese Orchestra, *Chinese Music*, **7**, 33 (1984).

Shen, Sin-yan, The Responsibilities of the Chinese Music Community to Mankind, *Chinese Music*, **8**, 63 (1985).

Shen, Sinyan, Acoustics of Ancient Chinese Bells, *Scientific American*, **256**, 94 (1987).

Shen, Sin-yan, Acoustics of Ancient Chinese Bells (in Japanese), *Scientific American* (Tokyo), **17**, 104 (1987).

Shen, Sin-yan, On the Acoustical Space of the Chinese Orchestra (in Chinese), *People's Music*, 1989, No. 2, 2 (1989).

Shen, Sin-yan, On the System of Chinese Fiddles I, *Chinese Music*, **13**, 24 (1990).

Shen, Sin-yan, On the System of Chinese Fiddles II, *Chinese Music*, **13**, 44 (1990).

University of California at San Diego Arts & Lectures, Program Notes by Shen Sin-yan for the Silk and Bamboo Ensemble, March 9, 1990 (1990).

Shen, Sin-yan, Making Chinese Music Totally Accessible - Our Contributions to Creating the World-Class Music of the 21st Century, *Chinese Music*, **19**, 4 (1996).

Shen, Sin-yan, Music For the Mind Versus Consumer Music: Is Chinese Music Different? *Chinese Music*, **22**, 44 (1999).

Are There Rules for Performance?

One of the best *erhu* players in Shanghai asked me "Is there a simple rule on when to use, and when not to use what type of vibrato?" This also bring up the question of the scores, on what is notated and what is not? As you may know, *erhu* vibrato is extremely complex, but not without rules. Primarily because of the freedom of the strings that are not supported by a fingerboard, the *erhu* vibratos can be generally classified into tension-altering vibrato and rolling vibrato. In *erhu* classics such as "Wailful Wrath by the River" there is further the deliberate use of vibrato contrast: on specific notes vibrato is heavily used, on other notes vibrato is lightly used, while on some notes no vibrato is used. Most players, however, play by experience. They understand the requirements of the cultural acoustics by heart, but have no theory.

My answer to the question is a simple one: musical interests are based on harmonic contrast. For example, in "Wailful Wrath by the River", the use of vibrato is based on contrast between the *zhi* harmony and the *yu* harmony. The *zhi* controls sol, do, and re. The *yu* controls la, re, and mi. The contrast between the two groups is clearly artistically very desirable. As you have heard from me time and time again, in

Chinese music, songs with distinctly different melodic lines which sound totally different to the outside world, may sound the same to the Chinese, because, as a thorough analysis will show, the melodic lines of these particular songs were formed by members of the very "same series of harmonies". A class of music like "The Old Six Measures (Lao Liuban)" thus offer the harmonic framework for composition, providing incredible room for creativity, yet staying within the same recognizable class of "Six Measures".

This brings us back to the importance of understanding the role of harmonic preferences in Chinese music. Instrumental performance, singing, and theatrical articulation are governed by harmony and the Chinese language. In instrumental music, since no vocal articulation is present, the freedom in expression is the greatest, and the role of harmonic contrast becomes the highest. In fact, there are many instrumental movements which are for the sole purpose of ascertaining intervals and acoustics, Li Yongnian on his *yueqin*, for example, produced the following

resonating acoustics, that is strictly speaking not melodic. The rule here is again based on a deep understanding of Chinese culture.

China was where the first music notation was developed and passed down. In folk and classical Chinese music, oral tradition and scores have always coexisted. At the same time, Chinese scores were never restrictive to imagination and creative - the case and point is the unnotated parts. Until very recently when western orchestral scores arrived, Chinese single instrument music was never fully notated, allowing for embellishments and variation according to players and environment, while orchestral scores permitted even greater extent of improvised performance. Thus sometime silk and bamboo is called Shanghai jazz[1] in the west. In reality it's not just silk and bamboo that improvises in Chinese musical art. Across the board Chinese ensemble music and solo music are among the most improvised in the world. The art of improvisation has been around for so long in China that most people do not pay special attention to it[2]. The general concept begins with the timeless notations whereby a dapu process is used to determine what gocs into the performance. I have called these

---

[1] During the 1970s and the 1980s when the Silk & Bamboo Ensemble of the Chinese Music Society of North America first performed in North America and Europe, the music community and critics likened their art form to jazz, and passionately called it "Shanghai Jazz".

[2] Unlike in the West, where so much of formal music is completely notated that improvisation in jazz and other music becomes specially noted.

scores "timeless" as they permit the fullest transmittal of a composition in time, through drastically different stylistic periods. This is possible primarily due to the importance of interval relations in Chinese compositions. Classical composition such as the "Lao Liuban" (Old Six Measure) merely provides the framework of interval series for the work. Embellishments and substitutions of individual notes by other members of the harmony used at the specific point in the "score".

Recent studies of children have produced results that point to the importance of ensemble sight reading at early age. First, with a group of children of similar age, players are provided with the right environment for focusing on a language, the musical language in this case that is instructed through the score. After sight reading once, the musical patterns are imprinted in the player's mind, making the second time around much easier. Such training in focusing one's attention and energy in music playing is recognized as some of the best ways to gain the discipline of learning. This points to the importance of score and ensemble playing. Other studies also point to the differences between regular children and specially musical children. When provided with a piano, regular children will bang on the key to produce noise, while the musical children will focus on getting the proper tone he or she desires out of, say, a singer note produced by a single finger - they will hear the tone and improve upon it. This points to the importance of hearing of music in musicianship. In Chinese music, both of these aspects are fully promoted. In silk and bamboo ensembles, little kids learn by playing in ensembles. The existence of scores guides the framework of the compositions, while kids learn by listening to many masters and hearing his or her own tones. In western ethnomusicology, there has been an overemphasis on the focus on oral traditions. This emphasis was important for obvious reason, since main stream classical music of the west does not use the oral tradition very much. When it comes to the study of Chinese music, however, the overemphasis of the oral tradition lightens the attention paid to artistic creativity inherent to the Chinese musical system - its intentionally simplified score, and its freedom for musicians to create unique performances. In fact, Chinese instrumental music is not intended for an audience. They are in reality only intended for music lovers and friends. Is their an audience for silk and bamboo? Sure there is. But the few members of the audience are there because they love the music making and desire to make similar music in the near future. Thus little kids would stick around older masters for ever, trying to get his or her attention, and eventually to benefit fully from his teaching. The future students usually demonstrate over a number of years their true quality and dedication to being a student and to the art form. They learn from the teachers everything from music to how to become a contributor to the art form. Most importantly, they learn from the teachers how to become a human being. Music making in China is a life-long process. Classical Chinese music is also a discipline in which musicians learn to become a full person. This, however, is not true of all musical art forms of China.

■

The New Posture of "The Mountain Village": On Zeng Jiaqing's Folk Music of Eastern China

"The Mountain Village" was quite a point of departure for me in musical thoughts. There was this little discussion one day in the early 1960s, on the fingering techniques required to play a fairly recently composed *erhu* solo entitled "The Mountain Village Gains New Posture". "The Mountain Village" was the work of Zeng Jiaqing. Today we know Zeng Jiaqing as the one composers who truly mastered folk music - the spirit of the folk music of a specific part of Eastern China. His two hugely successful *erhu* solo "The Mountain Village" and "Going to the Fair" were some of the greatest masterpieces based in folk music[1] rather than on folk music. In many instances, Chinese composers who used folk music merely recognized the melodic skeleton or the melodies themselves in creating new works, which were not creative most of the time. Zeng Jiaqing, however, transformed these folk music-based acoustics into works that truly capture the cultural backdrop and musical spirit of related original works in

[1] Notice I do not say his works are based on folk music. They are so completely deep-rooted in the music of Jiangsu and Anhui he is familiar with that they are truly based in folk music.

the tradition of Jiangsu and Anhui. "Going to the Fair" and "The Mountain Village Gains New Posture" are quite different compositions. "Going to the Fair" is fully recognizable as "Wang Sanjie Goes to the Fair" from Anhui. "Wang Sanjie Goes to the Fair" is a complete folk song with many verses. The music follows a young lady Wang Sanjie's physical and emotional movements on her way to the fair. The music's ups and downs are musically and otherwise completely in sink with her emotional changes, set in a typical Eastern farming community environment. "The Mountain Village", however, generates the most misunderstandings. Its happy country tune, in Chinese Shang modality, is often confused as being a very sad tune by Western listeners[2]. "Mountain Village" places in the hands of the *erhu* performer a detailed and full depiction of the true joy of residents of a mountain village, usually very poor and who never leave the village, upon exciting changes to the village - thus the appearance of "New Posture" in the title. The true joy here is in the glissando of the first and second finger on the left hand and in the breathing on the bowing on the right hand. The overall tonal space of the *erhu* and the *yangqin* controls the musical psychology of the audience throughout. Replacing the *erhu* and the *yangqin* by other instruments or by an orchestra would not do justice to the work as genuine Chinese music.

---

[2] This is a problem of cultural acoustics. Cultural acoustics manifests most prominently in interval space. When ears trained in Western music hear "The Mountain Village Gains New Posture", the fourth and fifth relation in shang harmony is modified by the brain to sound like third and fifth.

This little discussion I started to talk about had to do with the question of "How do you know which fingering to use where in the Mountain Village?" Among our *erhu* players, the consensus was "You really didn't have to know!" It just came naturally as you played. This is the situation with such folk pieces. Once you understood the culture of the music, once you are feeling it, you naturally know what to do! It implies no easy theory needs to be written down. This is not entirely true, of course. In theory, such cultural phenomenon can be translated into physical requirements which can be classified. A theory[3] on "Mountain Village" fingering is thus completely doable. This little discussion, though, shows a number of important points. When you are dealing with cultural acoustics, immersion provides natural means of problem solving. This is however not true with many other types of folk music that are less emotionally taxing. But when you have a master like Zeng Jiaqing writing for you, it is not the case of "catching the essence" anymore - you have the full and entire thing.

Today, all over the world, we see composers trying to capture some essence of a certain aspect of world music. The results of most of these work are commercial music that don't look like much of anything at all musically. This is, however, not my main complaint. The main problem with these compositions are their low emotional and cultural content, and eventually low

---

[3] I do write down fingering details nowadays when teaching students. The point is though you don't really need to have them. When it sounds right, the fingering and bowing are correct.

musical interest. There is the other school which always talks about complete preservation of folk music. Such work is only important statistically - there must be sufficient samples, data points, for every generation of folk music, in order for us to fully document our music. Zeng Jiaqing is truly different from most other Chinese composers whose music I have come to know well. In the period 1960s through 1990s, I had the opportunity to play all of Zeng Jiaqing's *erhu* compositions in *erhu* concerts throughout the world. *Erhu* compositions today are full of modified folk tunes, but none of them has the level of fullness and maturity of Zeng Jiaqing's presentation of the true music of the areas in China he is most familiar with. I began this discussion with the fingering questions my *erhu* colleagues asked in the early days. These performance methods and artistic techniques are completely integral to the *erhu* music and folk music of these Eastern regions of China. Thirty years later, I am convinced "Going to the Fair" and "The Mountain Village" are the best pieces for anyone to learn Chinese folk music from, especially folk music of the Jiangsu and the Anhui areas. I have played Jiangnan silk and bamboo all my life. Coming from somewhat similar areas in Eastern China even by Chinese standards, Zeng Jiaqing's music is entirely different. It represents the Chinese music that is not covered by silk and bamboo at all here.

■

Chinese Classical Art Songs & Their Impacts

Chinese art music has its roots in pure instrumentals of the scholarly community. The major developments in pure instrumental artistry occurred on silk strings. By the end of the Song period, however, this classical music had seriously declined. The "Da Yue Yi" (A Critical Review of Classical Music) and "Qin Se Gaogu Tu" (An Anthropological & Iconographical Review of the Qin and the Se) of Jiang Kui (Jiang Baishi, 1155?-1221?) during the Southern Song period critiqued the loss in understanding of *qin-se*[1] music and classical music during his time. He was inspired by the literary giant Xin Qiji (1140-1207)[2], and both were disappointed with the overall decline of

---

[1] Qin-Se music featured pure instrumentals using the classical silk string instruments of qin, se, ruan and others.

[2] Xin Qiji lived at a time when General Yue Fei (1103-1141) was just murdered by Emperor GaoZong (Zhao Gou) and Qin Kuai who did not want Yue Fei and his army to further protect the Song from the Jin (Nuzhen) army and who were inclined to surrender. When Xin was born in Jinan, Shandong, Yue Fei was to be killed two years later, Jinan was under Jin rule for 12 years, and the Song capital of Bianjing (Kaifeng, Henan) had been lost to the Jin for 14 years.

the Song Dynasty. Xin is known as one of the greatest ci[3] writers. Xin Qiji and Jiang Kui lived at a time when the Chinese court was under severe and constant pressure from northern invaders. Reacting to Song's decline, in 1199 Jiang composed 14 songs accompanied by orchestra for the Song court, aiming at saving Song from further military and political decline - his compositions aimed at raising the morale of the Song army. His most important contribution, however, was in the series of 28 art songs that are still studied by all Chinese musicologists today. His best known 17 art songs were notated in suzipu (common character score, a form of gongchipu). His 10 "Yue Jiu Ge" were notated in luluzipu (scores using lu-lu characters). His *qin* songs were notated in jianzipu, used widely in horizontal zither *qin* music[4]. This tradition of art songs is treasured today in, for example, newly composed vocal music based in Tang poetry. Liu Wenjin's "Yellow Crane Tower: Seeing Meng Haoran off to Guangling" based on the poem by Li Bai (701-762) is one such excellent work.

---

[3] Ci is poetry writing to specific tunes with strict tonal patterns and rhyme schemes, in fixed numbers of lines and words. Music lyrics is also called ci. Ci poetry originated in broadly recognized format in the Tang period (618-907) and was representative of the largest quantity of literary work in the Song period (960-1279). The names of the tunes to which ci poems are composed is cipai.

[4] The qin (fingerboard zither) has two to three hundred notations for tonal requirement in performance artistry the score of which is jianzipu (meaning score of simplified characters), and qin musicians are continuously generating more as needs arise. Tone is the most desired quality in musical interpretation for a large category of Chinese music. It is part of the melodic flow.

Recent art songs in the 20th century were almost composed exclusively during the war years. In 1938, trumpet artist Xia Zhiqiu organized the Wuhan Hechang Tuan (The Wuhan Choir) to travel to Southeast Asia, to raise funds for the war of resistance. In 1939 he met tenor Huang Yuanyin in Singapore. At the time Xia was writing "Sixiang Qu" (Remembering Homeland). The melody of this art song was inspired by ballad singing Xia had himself heard in Marcau, and the final lyrics for "Remembering Homeland" were written by Dai Tiandao according to Xia's composition. Xia eventually wrote it for Huang Yuanyin to sing. Huang made this now well-known classic popular when he was only 18. Nine years later in 1948 Huang Yuanyin recorded "Zhuixun" (In Search) in Hong Kong for the French-owned Baidai Records. "In Search" was written by the famed composer Liu Xue-an[5] and its lyrics was by Xu Jianwu. "In Search" expresses the longing for true love, and for perpetual light and illumination. At the time of the composition, China was under such darkness for its people and intellectuals, that many composers looked for light and future brightness in their work. Xu Jianwu and Liu Xue-an were in search of light and illumination, and Liu Tianhua, the *erhu* master, was in search of brightness. "In Search" had such an impact on me when I was younger, that I continued to perform it in the United States. Today I find its contents still applicable. One integral component of all art song's success is in the instrumental parts. Liu Wenjin's

---

[5] Liu Xue-an is best known for "Changcheng Yao" (Song of the Great Wall).

"Seeing Meng Hoaran off to Guangling"[6] is probably the best composed Chinese song for voice and a small Chinese orchestra. It was in this piece that listeners realized the importance and power of the classic round lute the *ruan*. The overall cultural acoustics of "Seeing Meng Haoran off to Guangling" is so genuinely Chinese classical that no imitations have come even close, to this very special category of Chinese musical art.

Ren Guang's "Yu Guang Qu" (Song of the Fishermen's Light, see next page) was a popular movie theme song of the 1930s. In 1932 Ren Guang was appointed Director of the Music Department at the Baidai Records in Shanghai. During this time he recorded many songs by Nie Er. Ren Guang also directed the small Chinese orchestra of the Baidai Records. Some of the currently popular compositions such as "The Flowers are Blooming and the Moon is Full" and "Spring at Emerald Lake" were recorded by Ren Guang and his orchestra. His own best known composition during this period was "Song of the Fisherman's Light". On the historical recording Ren Guang personally played the piano accompaniment. In the 1970s Wu Hourui and I directed a successful series of performances featuring the choir version of "Song of the Fishermen's Light". When the LP recording was issued, the U.S. Library of Congress said it was the first record issued in the U.S. by a Chinese choir. I also recorded "Song of the Fishermen's Light" on the *erhu* with Lee Yuan-Yuan. It is perhaps my best loved song ever. The other favorite of similar period was Zhang Han-hui's "Songhuajiang Shang" (On the

---

6 Lyrics by Li Bai (701-762), the greatest Tang poet.

渔 光 曲

中速
1 云 儿 飘 在
2 东 方 现 出
pp
海 空， 鱼 儿 藏 在 水 中，
明， 星 儿 藏 入 天 空，
早 晨 太 阳 里 晒 鱼 网， 迎 面 吹 过 来
早 晨 渔 船 儿 返 回 程， 迎 面 吹 过 来
大 海 风
送 潮 风

Songhua River). For this historically important composition Zhang Han-hui was featured as a Musician of the Year during the 20th Century in the "Chinese Music" international journal by the Chinese Music Society of North America (CMSNA).

Another song that I continued to perform in the United States was of 20th Century literary vintage. The lyrics of Xu Zhimuo's "Ou Ran" (An Accidental Encounter) were set to a most successful musical creation of this century in this art song by Li Wei-ning. Xu, of course, is well known as the talented modern writer, who had many ups and downs in his love life, and the one to receive Tagore when Tagore visited China from India. "An Accidental Encounter" is among the best depiction of Xu Zhimuo's emotions in what he calls an accidental encounter.

During the 1930s and the 1940s, many concerts featured "The River Flows East" and "I live at the Source of the Yangzi River". During the 1950s these songs were heard from Singapore to Taipei[7]. I consider "I live at the Source of the Yangzi" one of the best written Chinese art songs ever, and it was by Qing Zhu. Qing Zhu's music is in the spirit of Xin Qiji's ci. Qing Zhu was a member of the 1911 Revolution. His name means "The Master of the Blue Sky". His full artistic name was Li Qing Zhu, and Li is a common Cantonese family name, and in this case "Li" meant "the ordinary people". His chosen musical name shows a great deal of his feelings for the ordinary Chinese people.

---

[7] The Chinese mainland was undergoing a dramatic political transformation at the time, and the works of Qing Zhu were not heard.

Qing Zhu was educated in Germany, with majors in law, piano, and composition theory, and he had a wonderful musician wife Hua Li Si whom he married from abroad. As far as we know Hua Li Si was a constant source of encouragement for Qing Zhu in times of difficulty. Qing Zhu was a musical pioneer and one of the most accomplished in Chinese art song writing. In theoretical understanding, artistic interest, and depth of composition, Qing Zhu (1893-1959) was one of the most accomplished art song composers of China in the 20th Century, and is one who had not been adequately recognized.

Qing Zhu's "The River Flows East" was based on the poem by Su Dongpuo and shows his passion for the "elegant and classy personalities of a thousand years". His best composition was, of course, "I Live at the Source of the Yangzi".

Qing Zhu was born Liao Shangguo, native of Huiyang County in Guangdong. He joined the 1911 Revolution at the age of 18. When he returned from Germany in 1922, Qing Zhu served at the Huangpu Military Academy. In 1929 he starting teaching as a Professor at the Shanghai Conservatory. He was a known theoretician. Theoretical works included "On Music", "Rudiments of Music" and several dozen commentaries and notes on music. He translated some works on musical aesthetics after 1949. His "I live at the Source of the Yangzi River" and "The River Flows East" are the best known. His "Lian Ru Hua" (Face Like Flower) is another outstanding composition I have conducted in the 1970s.

Among composers I have come to be in contact with, Qing Zhu (1893-1959) was one of the most accomplished art song composers of China in the 20th Century, and is one who had not been adequately recognized. His "Wuo[8] Zhu Changjiang Tou" (I live at the Source of the Yangzi) is an incredibly moving song

I Live at the Source of the Yangzi

[8] Of course, strict transliteration would call for "wo" in these songs, but importance of the articulation of "I" is better served by breaking up the inflection into "wuo".

with a formidable structure. Its lyrics are so closely knit with the piano accompaniment, its paragraphing is so dramatic and yet emotions subtle, that it creates the ultimate excitement in the listener. Each time I hear it performed, the accompaniment of "I Live at the Source of the Yangzi" sticks to the voice of the vocal soloist. The imagery in the lyrics by Li Zhi-yi[9] is also absolutely incredible. Once again the poetry form of ci is used here. It begins with "I live upstream on the Yangzi River, and you live downstream on the Yangzi...." and the female personality continues to feel the presence of her love who lives downstream - "I think of you everyday but cannot see you. We drink the same Yangzi water...."

This lyric is out of this world, but the effect of the song for soprano truly transcends the words and reflects Qing Zhu's musical might. His music implied his passion and incredible determination, despite the worse of hard times. As he would say, "The tears between the lines could never be printed!" He probably felt he was unable to drastically reverse the trend of negative happenings, he used the best in ancient poetry to musically express his own power, which turned out to be huge. I consider Qing Zhu among the most talented musicians in the 20th Century.

Art songs for mixed voices and choral compositions of the last Century receive mixed reviews from me. A few exceptions

---

[9] Li Zhi-yi was a Song Dynasty poet and "Wuo Zhu Changjiang Tou" (I live at the Source of the Yangzi) was written in the ci format, the favorite of Song period poets.

include "Sen-lin A! Lu-se De Hai-yang" (Oh Forests! - You Ocean of Green) by Chen Tianhe, and "Tianlun Ge" (Song of Family Bonding) originally composed by Huang Zi and rearranged for mixed choir. "Oh Forests!" is a large composition devoted to reforestation, environmental protection and soil conservation. Its mixed choir effects and solo parts are both spectacular and the whole piece powerful. "Family Bonding", like "Song of the Fishermen's Light", was written for a movie and became quite popular and is well known to many 20th Century Chinese. The Ohio State University Chinese Choir and the Northwestern University Chinese Choir were the first to record these classic choral compositions in the United States[10].

A number of Chinese singers entered the voice profession with a clear mission to save Chinese culture, as the true Chinese intellectual is always passionate about history and art[11]. The great tenor Sheng Jialun of the 20th Century systematically collected scores of instrumental music during his lifetime. Sheng, of course, was the artist featured in the famous theme song from the movie "The Midnight Voice (Yeban Gesheng)". "The Midnight voice was composed by Xian Xinghai[12] and the song was made nationally and internationally famous by the

---

[10] Recordings made in the 1970s in Columbus, Ohio, New York, and in Chicago.

[11] As Confucius said, "The burden on the gentleman is lifelong."

[12] Composer of "The Yellow River Cantata". Passages of the Cantata were later used in the work "Yellow River Piano Concerto".

incredibly beautiful voice of Sheng Jialun and his commitment to Chinese musical arts.

Sheng Jialun, like many Chinese intellectuals, was passionately involved in a historical mission to preserve and propagate Chinese culture. Throughout his life, he collected *guqin*[13] scores from book vendors on the streets of China. Sheng Jialun was incredibly talented as a musician as well, making him an ideal propagator of Chinese music and songs such as "The Midnight Voice".

[13] The *qin* is also called *guqin*. The fingerboard zither is one of the most important classical instruments. It is also the instrument on which Chinese scholars cultivate their individual temperaments.

■

Zhang Han-Hui and "On the Songhua River"

Born in the Year of the Tiger, Zhang Han-hui is perhaps the most celebrated composer for popular patriotic songs in this century. In 1936 he wrote "On the Songhua River" (Songhua Jiang Shang). To date no other song has surpassed its popularity among the generation of the 20th Century. Zhang was a theater major.

Many of us remember "On the Songhua River" as a young person. The Songhua River runs through the Northeast of China and signifies the large area that was taken from the Chinese people by Japanese invaders in the beginning of the Japanese Invasion. In 1936, Zhang Han-hui wrote "On the Songhua River" (*Songhua Jiang Shang*). "Wuo di Jia .... zai Dongbei Songhua Jiang Shang ...." (My home .... is on the Songhua River in the Northeast....) is the perpetually popular phrase from "Songhua Jiang Shang" (On the Songhua River). As we review music of the 20th Century, "On the Songhua River" puts modern patriotic songs on the map among the common people. There are many patriotic songs by Liu Xue-an, Nie Er, Xian Xinghai, Huang Zhi, and numerous others. But Zhang Han-hui's "*Songhua Jiang Shang*" has its special position.

The best known song of the 1930s and the 1940s to all Chinese of that generation was "*Songhua Jiang Shang*" (On the Songhua River), written for vocal solo, and set in the backdrop of the Japanese invasion of the Chinese Northeast. Using the famous lead phrase of "My home - is on the Songhua River", Zhang Han-hui (1092-1946) composed this all-time favorite patriotic song. There were a huge number of vocal compositions during the contiguous periods of the Sino-Japanese War, the Second World War, and the Chinese civil war. "*Songhua Jiang Shang*" is one that left imprints on everyone. Even after 1949, it was sung and loved by ordinary people and music lovers both on the Chinese mainland and on Taiwan. The generation that moved from the Chinese mainland to Taiwan remembered vividly this popular song's impact on their generation. For a while (the 1950s through the 1970s) the song was altered a bit and sung on Taiwan. Later the original version was approved for public performance on Taiwan. This story shows the vitality of a truly popular song which left imprints on every citizen!

"On the Songhua River" sings about the enormous natural resource in the Chinese Northeast, and describes the huge pain Japanese occupation of Shenyang on the Eighteenth of September ("Jiu Yi Ba") has inflicted on the Chinese population. It sings about love for parents and love for one's country. In a plain but dramatically articulated language, Zhang Han-hui captured the moment and the spirit of the generation.

What kind of a musician was Zhang Han-hui? Zhang Han-hui learned and played the *erhu* (the python-skin second fiddle), the *pipa* (the pear-shaped grand lute played with five-finger strum), the *sanxian* (the long-necked finger-board python-skin lute) and other traditional instruments with his father in Dingxian County of Hebei Province (You may recall that Dingxian County is home to a number of fairly well known traditional instrumental ensembles, such as the Ziwei Village Chuige Ensemble), during the formative period of his musical training in his youth. "*Songhua Jiang Shang*" benefitted from his other training. In college, Zhang Han-hui formally studied theater, at the Beijing Arts Academy during the years 1925-1929. After the Academy he worked as an actor, composer, and writer. His strong musical, literary, and theatrical background allowed him to effectively write patriotic songs (He usually wrote both the lyrics as well as the music for each vocal composition). "On the Songhua River" has highly dramatic impacts on its listeners. The singer needs to be a good singer and an excellent theatrical performer at the same time, to grasp its emotional content. Zhang Han-hui's musical talents and his theatrical training and experience both contributed to the success of this vocal masterpiece. The backdrop of the war years also shaped its display of national pride and enormous strength and integrity.

What is in a name? Composer Zhang Han-hui's name has a special meaning. "Han" means "cold". "Hui" means "brightness and warmth". The combination probably implies he would bring brightness and warmth to a cold environment, or that in cold periods one saw light and warmth. His name is certainly fitting. During the low points in recent Chinese history, his songs and music brought life and strength to the Chinese people. Chinese culture is one in which parents embody their hopes into a child's given name, though there are also frequent changes of names, and the adoption of an academic or scholarly name, or a sign.

During his life, Zhang Han-hui composed a total of more than fifty songs. Good recording of many of these songs of the first half of this century are hard to come by any more. But a good recording of "*Songhua Jiang Shang*" appears in the film "The East is Red" which is widely available in the U.S. and in Europe.

■

Fun With the Burgandian: Music of the Yuan Dynasty

In the 1980s the Chinese Music Society of North America co-produced a series of programs with an early music pioneer group the Burgandian Consort. For the joint series the Silk & Bamboo Ensemble played in silk and bamboo style complete with period repertoire, in conjunction with the Burgandian Consort, which played Italian and other European music on early music instruments, from either similar or slightly later periods in Europe. This series was great fun for all the musicians and the audiences. Its theme was focused on East and West exchanges in music historically. The series was quite a success with our broader U.S. audience. In designing the series, I worked closely with music director Rick Simons of the Consort. Our initial focal point was the personality Marco Polo, who visited China during the Yuan dynasty. This was initially Rick's idea. Yuan was the dynasty in China established by the descendants of the famous Genghis Khan. Marco Polo on the other hand, according to the Marco Polo Memoir, interacted extensively on his trips with the Yuan court and the Chinese people in several Eastern and Northern provinces. There were at that point in history quite a large number of Europeans like him who had come to China and traded with Chinese businesses. Polo, however, was not the first one who did what he did. In fact, he heard so much, when he was younger, from others that he became so attracted that he had to come to China. There were in recent times scholars in the West who were not completely convinced whether Polo existed, or whether Polo himself actually went to China, and who thought Polo could have produced material for his Memoir which was a transcription of what he said, using everything he had heard from other travellers and business men, who did travel to China. For our historical music series it therefore made great sense to focus on the silk & bamboo compositions which became popular in the Yuan period and was new and popular then. The Yuan period was established by the descendants of Genghis Khan. They used the name "Yuan" as it signifies an origin. The Yuan dynasty wanted to start anew for China. Thus China, in a sense, gained a new origin in that period. The Yuan period saw a huge boom in international trade, and Chinese cities were highly prosperous. Instrumental music and theatrical music, as a result, really took off as popular art forms of the people. Silk and bamboo music boomed in the Yuan dynasty. The classics "Xingjie" (Processional), "Liuban" (The Six Measures) all appeared in this period as popular ensemble pieces. When Marco Polo arrived, he saw a prosperous China in which there were a thousand cultural practices the Italians could have been excited about. Food preparation and culinary art, for instance, caught his eyes. He also became fascinated by the vertical fiddles - the huqin - in the Chinese army. The vertical fiddles used horse-haired bows which were not seen in Europe at the time. This became a point of close connection and a point of exchange between the bowed string of China and later the bowed string of Italy and Europe.

When the Yuan dynasty was established, intellectuals were seriously discriminated against, while commerce boomed. The sectors of economy became constantly in search of entertainment. During this time art music disappeared completely but theatrical music made head way. Going to the theater was like going to the movie - a common mode of relaxation. While brilliant playwrights put moral stories on stage, the central philosophy of Chinese music declined. The impact of this period lasts till today.

As you know, instrumental music as a genre was non-existent in Europe in the middle ages. In the last few centuries, it grew as accompaniments to dance, social functions, and musical shows[1]. This was totally opposite to what went on in China. In China, art music was established in the Spring & Autumn period, the times of philosophers. The decline of the Song dynasty served as a line of demarkation for the decline of art music.

Large cities in China became huge during the boom of the Tang period, following an unprecedented economic boom. Cities became commerce and population centers. City citizens became a large sector of chinese society, and as a result, ballad singing,

[1] During the hundred years between 1450 and 1550, distinct styles, genres, and forms of instrumental music emerged in Europe. Independent instrumental music existed earlier, in the form of dances, fanfare, and the like. See Grout & Palisca, 1996.

which was one of the favorite forms of entertainment, took off in popularity. Going into the Song dynasty, ballad singing not only dominated much of city life, it also became a favorite form of entertainment in the farming villages.

During the 13th Century, the Mongolians swallowed Jin and Song, and invaded Europe, making China the most powerful country in the world, militarily and economically. Before this time, the main stream of foreign trade took place on ocean routes, but now global trade was taking place. The centralization of population in large cities became acute, and the large number of ordinary citizens required much daily entertainment. The "zaju" was the theatrical art form which evolved from ballad singing. It first occurred in the North. During the Yuan dynasty, citizens were ranked according to profession into ten categories, and intellectuals were ranked the ninth, below prostitutes and barely above beggars. This was how they were seriously discriminated for political reasons. As a result of this situation, brilliant literary writers imbedded themselves into the theatrical profession, working with ballad singers and actors, as playwrights (see e.g. Zhang & Guo, 1980). The "zaju" was accompanied by strings known collectively as xiansuo[2]. Today the art of the northern fiddles is still a highly treasured part of instrumental music.

---

[2] This term, xiansuo, is still used today for Northern string music. The Thirteen Suites for Xiansuo, for example, uses a string quartet format, with three tantiao plucked strings and one bowed string.

Polo[3] was highly impressed by the Chinese fiddles. String instruments prominent at the time includes the *matouqin* (the horse head fiddle[4]), the *sanxian* (the fingerboard lute with three strings and no frets), the *zheng* (the horizontal open-string zither), the *pipa* (the grand lute), the *xiqin* (the vertical fiddle and the supporting fiddle), the fingerboard vertical fiddles, and other skin fiddles and wood fiddles. He said "In Kublai Khan's army, there were these fabulous fiddles played with horse haired bows..." He was indeed so impressed that when he dictated to Rustichello of Pisa in Genoa prison, the Chinese vertical fiddles stood out in his memory.

While having fun with the Burgandians, I had an opportunity to review what happened musically in the Yuan period.

For concert locations in this special historical music series, we utilized both temples and churches of excellent acoustics. The

---

[3] Nicolo Polo, his 17 year old son, Marco, and his brother, Maffeo, left Acre about November, 1271, on their journey by way of the ancient Silk Trade Route to Shangtu and arrived more than three years later. For 17 years the Polos remained high in the Khan's favor. In 1292 they had the opportunity to accompany a young woman who was to become the wife of the Khan of Persia to Tabriz. From Persia, they went by way of Constantinople to Venice, arriving home towards the end of 1295. In 1298 Marco Polo was captured by the Genoese in a naval attack on Venice and was taken to a Genoa prison. During the year's confinement a fellow prisoner, Rustichello of Pisa, wrote down Marco's experiences at his dictation.

[4] Originally known as the dragon-head fiddle. The head of the *matouqin* could either take the shape of a dragon head or a horse head.

Unity Temple we used was designed by Frank Lloyd Wright with ideal acoustical properties for the purpose of our acoustical performances. It was also built by someone whose deep exposure to both Eastern and Western architecture and arts shaped his aesthetics.

Our relation with the Burgandian persisted during the series and afterwards. It is one of joint exploration and true friendship. One member of the Burgandian later joined our Chinese Classical Orchestra (CCO). During this important collaboration, we explored each other's art forms and played each other's music, played together, and we dialogued together with our captivated audience. We also appeared on Studs Terkel[5] together. The Burgandian musicians are true lovers of their instruments: bowed strings, lutes, and winds. Most of the instruments used in the Series were hand-made by the Burgandian musicians. With the fabulous Burgandian arrangements, Chinese music including the classic "Autumn Moon over the Han Palace" sounds genuinely exciting acoustically on these recreated early European instruments, which we found to be true cousins of Chinese musical instruments.

---

[5] Studs Terkel, the greatest interviewer and Pulitzer Prize Winner, has interviewed personalities in all fields, in more than 50 years and thousands of interviews. He spent 45 years on WFMT, the most important classical music station, in Chicago.

REFERENCES

Grout, D.J. and C.V. Palisca, *A History of Western Music*, Norton, New York (1996).

Lu E-Ting, *Kunju Yanchu Shigao* (Historical Notes on Kun Opera Performance, in Chinese), Shanghai Literary Press (1980).

Simons, Richard A., Reflections Related to the Arrangement of Autumn Moon over the Han Palace for Medieval Western Musical Instruments, *Chinese Music*, 15, 44 (1992)

Zhang Gen and Guo Han-cheng, *Zhongguo Xiqu Tongshi* (A General History of Chinese Theater, in Chinese), China Theater Press (1980).

INDEX

Deep is the Night, 77

Hong Xian Steals the Box, 57

ABOUT THE AUTHOR

Born in 1949 to Shanghainese parents, Sin-yan Shen studied music at very early age, mastering the vertical fiddle family of instruments. His dual career in music and physics culminated in the development of cultural acoustics, a discipline addressing scientifically the cultural molding of our ears and brain when it comes to music. Dr. Shen's life-long work centers on the question of "what music really is?" His teaching in North America and abroad has created a new understanding of music, its creative and social functions, and provides inspiration to a new generation of composers and music practitioners.

Dr. Sin-yan Shen pioneered the teaching of cultural acoustics at Northwestern and Harvard. He is currently Music Director of the Silk and Bamboo Ensemble and the Chinese Classical Orchestra, both touring internationally under the auspices of the Chinese Music Society of North America. He is editor of the international journal *Chinese Music*, music authority for the Encyclopedia Britannica, and a Fulbright Scholar. He serves as Technical Advisor to the Shanghai Musical Instruments Factory.

http://chinesemusic.net

ORDER FORM

Chinese Music
Monograph Series

■ ***PLEASE ENTER MY ORDER***

■ **FAX: +1 630-910-1551**

Name____

Street____

____

City______________________________State________Zip code______________

Country____________________________________

qty	Book Title	Price	Total
	CHINESE MUSIC AND ORCHESTRA: A primer on Principles and Practice	$17.95	
	CHINESE MUSICAL INSTRUMENTS **NEW!**	$22.95	
	CHINA: A Journey into Its Musical Art **NEW!**	$22.95	
	CHINESE MUSIC IN THE 20TH CENTURY (available in November, 2000)	$22.95	
	Shipping & Handling: $3.50, Foreign $4.50 / book (Add $1.00 for each additional copy)		
	TOTAL :	US$	

■ METHOD OF PAYMENT
☐ Check or Money Order. (in US funds please)
Credit Card: ☐ VISA ☐ MasterCard ☐ Discover ☐ AMEX

Credit Card____ Exp. Date:______/______

Signature____________________________Tel:__________/______________

■ Send to **Chinese Music Society**, PO Box 5275, Woodridge, IL 60517-0275 USA Tel: 630-910-1551 FAX: 630-910-1561 ■